Paddle Maryland

Other Guides by Bryan MacKay

Hike Maryland
Cycle Maryland

Paddle
MARYLAND

A GUIDE to Rivers, Creeks, and Water Trails

Bryan MacKay

Photographs by Debi and Bryan MacKay

Maps by Bill Nelson

JOHNS HOPKINS UNIVERSITY PRESS · BALTIMORE

© 2018 Johns Hopkins University Press
All rights reserved. Published 2018
Printed in the United States of America on acid-free paper
9 8 7 6 5 4 3 2 1

Johns Hopkins University Press
2715 North Charles Street
Baltimore, Maryland 21218-4363
www.press.jhu.edu

Library of Congress Cataloging-in-Publication Data

Names: MacKay, Bryan, author.
Title: Paddle Maryland : A Guide to Rivers, Creeks, and Water Trails /
    Bryan MacKay ; Photographs by Debi and Bryan MacKay ; Maps by Bill Nelson.
Description: Baltimore : Johns Hopkins University Press, 2018. |
    Includes index.
Identifiers: LCCN 2017030364| ISBN 9781421425023 (pbk. : alk. paper) |
    ISBN 1421425025 (pbk. : alk. paper) | ISBN 9781421425030 (electronic) |
    ISBN 1421425033 (electronic)
Subjects: LCSH: Canoes and canoeing—Maryland—Guidebooks. | Kayaking—
    Maryland—Guidebooks. | Maryland—Guidebooks.
Classification: LCC GV776.M3 M33 2018 | DDC 797.12209752—dc23
    LC record available at https://lccn.loc.gov/2017030364

A catalog record for this book is available from the British Library.

*Special discounts are available for bulk purchases of this book. For more information,
please contact Special Sales at 410-516-6936 or specialsales@press.jhu.edu.*

Johns Hopkins University Press uses environmentally friendly book materials,
including recycled text paper that is composed of at least 30 percent post-consumer
waste, whenever possible.

Contents

Preface

Welcome to *Paddle Maryland*. This book is the culmination of my forty years of experience exploring the waterways of Maryland. During that time I've paddled both canoes and kayaks in twenty states, but my many fond memories always call me back to Maryland, my lifelong home. I love the narrow, twisting bald cypress swamps of the lower Eastern Shore, but I also love the pounding whitewater of the North Branch of the Potomac and the main stem Potomac at Harpers Ferry. And my go-to, close-to-home frequent paddle trip is on the clear, clean Upper Gunpowder between the reservoirs, forty minutes from my house. Maryland has an amazing diversity of rivers, creeks, and lakes suitable for a paddling trip, and the goal of this book is to share some of my favorites with you.

If you like exploring the more remote and hard-to-reach corners of the Free State, canoeing and kayaking offer you the chance to get to places few others can. Swamps and marshes, in particular, are virtually impossible to access on foot, and boats with motors can't get up into the really interesting narrow passageways of the headwaters. Similarly, rivers and streams rushing through steep-sided gorges cannot be seen except from river level. And the flora and fauna of these riparian corridors are often fascinating, with a special beauty all their own.

Maryland has many advantages for the paddler. Geographically, it extends from the ocean to the mountains, and both are within a three-hour drive of the majority of the state's residents. Chesapeake Bay, Maryland's most significant physiographic feature, has 11,684 miles of tidal shoreline, making it the largest estuary in the United States. The Potomac River, forming the state's entire southern boundary, is a superb recreational amenity for paddlers. Tucked away among the folds of the land are a variety of streams, creeks, and small rivers that drain into these two bodies of water, many suitable for wetting a paddle. Maryland is a progressive state in terms of conservation, and so much of the land surrounding these paddling venues is in public hands; this means that the view from the river is often of forests rather than housing tracts or industrial sites.

For this book I have selected my favorite places to paddle. Each has some outstanding characteristic that calls me to return again and again. Whether it's a remote river where you can experience a sense of solitude, a winding stream with exceptional wildflowers or wildlife, or just a scenic location best appreciated from water level, every trip is certain to delight you in some way. The text is designed to illuminate what makes these special places so interesting and valuable. In an era where much basic information is available online and social media promotes opinion unencumbered by expertise and experience, *Paddle Maryland* is a book whose added value lies in enlightening, descriptive text based on my decades of paddling experience.

I brought certain prejudices to the process of selecting the nearly two dozen paddling trips for this book. First, for tidal trips, I prefer small, narrow, twisting creeks. For the most part, they are more intimate, increase your chances of seeing wildlife, and cannot be accessed by motorboat. Unlike large bodies of water, which tend to be subject to wind, making canoeing (less so kayaking) more challenging, these sheltered channels provide calm waters. Second, for nontidal paddling trips, I have chosen rivers and streams that usually have enough water to paddle in during the warmer months of the year. These trips often require more paddling skill and experience. There may be hazards like rocks and downed trees in the river, and there's an increased likelihood that you may tip over and take a swim. For the most part, I do not include reservoirs; I find them boring to paddle.

Accompanying each trip description is an essay that considers a relevant organism or related concept in greater detail than I've provided in the trip description. New findings gleaned from the recent scientific literature enhance these life histories. Some of these essays provide a closer look at a particular aspect of conservation in Maryland, and they frequently provide a perspective on controversial issues with suggestions for future actions on the part of society.

Written directions at the end of each chapter will get you to the launch point from the Washington-Baltimore metropolitan area. A street address is included (where a usable one exists), as are GPS coordinates for the launch point. Note, however, that handheld GPS units are not always reliable in steep river valleys. Similarly, cell phone coverage is intermittent or nonexistent on some of these rivers, especially those in the western counties of Maryland. Should you get into trouble on a river, don't count on technology to get you out.

I hope you enjoy using this book as you explore Maryland by canoe or kayak. I wish you many safe and memorable experiences.

Acknowledgments

For more than forty years, paddling has been my favorite outdoor sport, and it remains so today. I am grateful to those paddlers who "showed me the ropes" years ago: how to paddle both canoe and kayak; how to be safe on the water, even in difficult whitewater; how to "read" the flow of a river; how to organize and lead a trip; how to tie a boat safely onto a car; and how to set an efficient car shuttle. These old friends include Warren Heppding, Phil Howard, Bob Davis, Tom Donohue, Chuck Gladding, Warren Therien, and Wil Gallager. I've enjoyed the companionship of dozens of paddlers over the years, mostly on trips with the Greater Baltimore Canoe Club (now the Baltimore Canoe and Kayak Club), especially Steve and Katy Meyer, Norm Fairhurst, Art and Chris Grace, Ken and Carolyn Loving, Pat McCauley, David Beck, Jim Broyles, April Foiles, Charlie Stine, Tricia Precht, and many others too numerous to mention. Tom Giannaccini deserves special thanks for paddling with me on a half dozen exploratory trips for this book in 2016. Mike McCrea turned me on to the subtle beauty of the Transquaking River, and the legendary Ed Gertler has always been a source of information and inspiration.

My wife, Debi MacKay, was new to paddling when she married me, but now she loves canoeing as much as I do. We've shared many a canoe, and canoe-in campsite, over the last fifteen years, and I am grateful for her good humor, resiliency, and enthusiasm. Debi has also contributed some of the photographs in this book, and for that I am thankful.

In 1992, a (fairly) young and definitely naïve version of me first approached Johns Hopkins University Press regarding possible publication of a guidebook to venues for hiking, cycling, and canoeing in Maryland. I am indebted to the Press and my long-time editor, Bob Brugger, for immediately accepting the manuscript and shepherding it through publication and sales. To date, that book has sold more than 21,000 copies, and it has been gratifying to receive so many compliments on it from people who love the outdoors. Now that book about the best places to go in Maryland for hiking, cycling, and paddling has received a fresh interpretation from the Press with the publication of three separate guidebooks, each devoted exclusively to a single sport. Each venue has been revisited, viewed with a fresh eye, and the text revised. New sites have been added. Information about nature has been updated. I believe these new books improve significantly on the older one; I have written the book I want to grab when I leave the house for a day of paddling. I appreciate my present editor at the Press, Catherine Goldstead, for her vision about this project and her steady hand at guiding it to fruition. I am grateful to Mary Lou Kenney for her proficiency with book production.

Maps for this book have been prepared by Bill Nelson of Bill Nelson Maps. I thank him for his expertise.

While any author receives and appreciates help with a writing project, he is ultimately responsible for any errors and omissions. Should you find any you wish to tell me about, I can be contacted through Johns Hopkins University Press.

River Days: A Perspective on Paddling Maryland Waterways

I've been paddling canoes and kayaks for more than forty years on rivers across Maryland and beyond. Some of my favorite memories are of paddling trips near and far, and some of my best friends I met decades ago on whitewater rivers. I love tiny, twisty swamp runs on the lower Eastern Shore, like the upper Pocomoke, once kept open by inmate work crews from the local jail but now terminally clogged with fallen trees. I love the Mather Gorge of the Potomac below Great Falls, where the power of even a summer-low river is evident in the boils and eddy lines and dynamic surfing waves. I love Sideling Hill Creek, an easy whitewater cruise in Washington County with its beautiful hemlock-hung rock outcrops, all the more treasured because it has sufficient water to paddle only a few days a year. But mostly I just love being outside, in a boat powered by my own arms, on a river that most Marylanders never get to see. As Ratty said in "The Wind in the Willows," there is "nothing—absolutely nothing, half so worth doing, as simply messing about in boats." I agree wholeheartedly. There are few things more magical than paddling silently and alone down a deserted river just to see what is around the next bend.

In those four decades, I've seen paddling evolve from a summer camp activity for kids and a sport for a tiny cadre of dedicated adults to a popular form of recreation enjoyed by large numbers of people of all ages and skill levels. This democratization of what was once a fringe pastime is the greatest change I've noticed in the paddling scene. And a welcome change it is, for without paddlers to enjoy them and advocate for them, rivers may sometimes run forgotten and neglected, mere natural sewers for our chemical pollutants and the detritus of civilization.

When I first picked up a paddle in the mid-1970s, there was a choice between a canoe and a kayak. Canoeing had a long and fabled history in North America; the voyageurs were responsible for exploring large parts of Canada, and Lewis and Clark used canoes for much of their journey to the Pacific and back. But neither the classic wood-and-canvas canoes of yesteryear nor the fragile fiberglass modern designs were well suited to the rocky nontidal rivers of the mid-Atlantic region. Canoe fabrication changed in the 1970s with the introduction of a material called ABS, setting a new standard for toughness and durability in a multifunctional hull design. To this day, I believe the Mad River Explorer to be the best all-around hull design. I've used (and abused) mine on windblown lakes in the Boundary Waters, weeklong canoe camping trips in the redrock canyons of Utah, and the boulder-strewn Class III rapids of the lower Yough.

In the early 1970s, kayaks were even less user-friendly than canoes. Most designs for river use were based on slight modifications of whitewater slalom kayaks, a sport enjoyed by only a few hundred stalwarts nationwide. These kayaks were constructed by hand, using fiberglass cloth and resin, a time-consuming, expensive, and difficult process. My first kayak was heavy, tippy, had a dangerously small cockpit and foot braces, and shed itchy fiberglass fibers with every use.

The first revolution in popularizing kayaking came without fanfare when a few companies figured out how to mold a kayak out of polyethylene plastic. Far more durable than fiberglass kayaks, plastic took over the market in just a few years. Nevertheless, designs continued to be based on whitewater boats, requiring a flexible "skirt" that sealed the paddler into the cockpit, and kayaking remained a fringe sport. What changed kayaking into a beginner-friendly, casual outdoor activity was the invention of mass-produced recreational kayaks: stable, short, plastic boats with open cockpits sold at attractive prices in big-box stores like Walmart and Dick's. In 2006, almost three times as many recreational kayaks were sold, as compared to canoes, and in 2014, more than 13 million recreational kayaks were sold. Drive to Ocean City on a summer weekend and it seems every third car sports one or more recreational kayaks on the same roof rack as the bicycles and beach chairs. Kayaking is no longer a fringe sport; it has achieved acceptance by families and individuals as an equal partner among their other fun toys.

But ultimately it doesn't matter what kind of kayak or canoe you own; the one you have available is the right one. What matters is that you use it, as often as possible, to get out on Maryland's beautiful rivers, estuaries, streams, and marshes, to reconnect with the natural world, to leave behind the bustle and cares of daily life, and to enjoy paddling through nature, over water, and under the dome of an infinite sky.

Paddle Maryland

Janes Island State Park

River Section: Janes Island State Park Marina to Flatcap beach and return
County: Somerset
Distance: About 1 mile of paddling, with the option of extending the trip for
as many as 12 miles: up to 3 miles of beachcombing
Difficulty: Easy, except when windy. Tidal flatwater
Hazards: Motorboat traffic, biting insects, wind
Tide Information: https://tidesandcurrents.noaa.gov/tide_predictions.html;
select Maryland and scroll to the Crisfield station
Highlights: A beautiful tidal salt marsh, a sandy beach perfect for beach-
combing, and expansive views of Chesapeake Bay
Nearby Canoe/Kayak Rental: Janes Island State Park, (410) 968-1565
More Information: Janes Island State Park, http://www.dnr.state.md.us
/publiclands/pages/eastern/janesisland.aspx, (410) 968-1565
Street Address: 2628 Alfred Lawson Drive, Crisfield, Maryland 21817
GPS Coordinates: 38.009057, 75.848038 (Janes Island marina launch site)

The meeting of land and water seems to create special places. Nowhere in Maryland is that juncture of land and water more gradual, more ephemeral, more changeable, than in the tidal marshes of the lower Eastern Shore. They are Maryland's version of the Everglades, where limitless vistas over shallow bays and low vegetation impart a sense of space and solitude. The absence of solid ground and the hordes of biting insects all conspire to keep humans at bay; these marshes may be the loneliest places in Maryland.

A good sense of these salt marshes can be experienced at Janes Island State Park, located just outside Crisfield in Somerset County. The park consists of a 310-acre developed mainland and a much larger island of low marshes and tidal guts separated from the mainland by a narrow channel. The mainland area contains a marina with boat rentals, picnic grounds, rental cabins, and more than 100 campsites, making it a fine base for exploration of the marsh. A channel leads through the center of the island to within 100 yards of the far shore, providing a sheltered waterway for paddlers. Once one is ashore, over two miles of sandy beach fronting on Tangier Sound invite beachcombing and swimming.

Trip Description

Launch your canoe or kayak from the state park marina, where there are wheelchair-accessible bathrooms, trash cans, a camp store, plenty of parking, a kayak launch dock, and motorboat, kayak, and canoe rentals. Paddle due west into Ward Creek, crossing Daugherty Channel, where you should watch out for fast-moving powerboats.

As you enter Ward Creek, the only high ground of Janes Island is on your left, featuring a loblolly pine forest. In the 1870s, at the southern tip of this island, a fish processing facility was established, an outlier of Crisfield, then known as the seafood capital of the world. All that remains now is a 50-foot-tall brick chimney, although there were once a boardwalk, a dance pavilion, and summer houses here.

As you paddle up Ward Creek, examine the mudflats lining the marsh on either side. The mud is convoluted, and it is honeycombed with tiny canals and tunnels. If the tide is low, you should be able to see dozens of fiddler crabs scurrying for shelter as you approach. Most are only two to three inches long, but the larger ones seem less skittish and may not enter their burrows if you keep your distance. Use binoculars to view the crabs. The males have one hugely oversized claw. It is used in courtship displays prior to mating, when the crab flexes and extends the pincer and waves the claw up and down. This display is also used to threaten other males competing for territory, but the claw is not an effective weapon despite its size. Fiddler crabs are among the most interesting residents of a marsh, but close observation of them will take time and quiet patience.

A thin layer of *Spartina alterniflora*, saltmarsh cordgrass, lines the channel. Farther back, where the ground is slightly higher, black rush dominates hundreds of acres of this marsh. This needlelike grass, about two feet high, often appears dead, lending it a blackish cast.

The deeply invaginated channels of Janes Island provide fine habitat for feeding herons and egrets. In summer, you'll certainly see

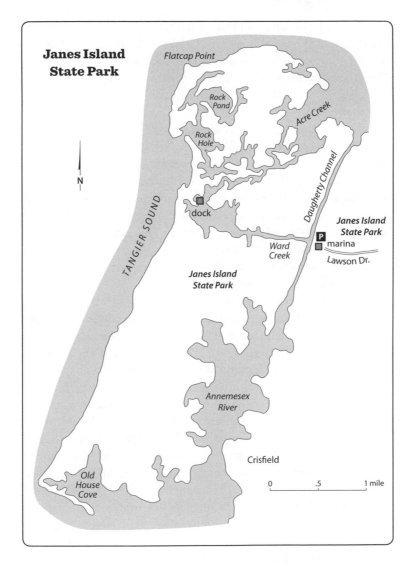

both snowy and American egrets, white, heronlike birds in small and large editions, respectively. The snowy egret has a black bill, whereas the American egret has a yellow one, a field mark that is easy to spot if you're unfamiliar with these common summer residents. Colored herons also come in two sizes, the larger great blue and the smaller green-backed. Great blue herons, which some people mistakenly call "cranes," are common along every watercourse in the state; they stand four feet high on stilt legs with long necks. The green-backed heron, although probably equally common, is more secretive, has shorter legs and neck, and typically stands about 16 inches high. All of these birds feed on minnows and other small fish that inhabit warm shallows at the water's edge; by running a seine net through these same waters, you too can get a feel for the richness and diversity of the piscine life of a salt marsh.

The channel widens after the first half mile. If you're uncertain of the proper direction, follow the numbered triangular channel markers. Your goal is a dock at the far end of the bay. It will be difficult to disembark from your canoe or kayak onto the dock, so beach your boat on a small sand spit to the left, haul it up well onto the sand so that it won't be floated off by a rising tide, and gather the necessary supplies for a beach walk. You'll definitely want to bring insect repellent between late May and first frost, along with sunscreen and whatever else you normally take to the beach.

Wade through the shallows from your landing site to the dock. The *Spartina* here houses a population of marsh periwinkles, small snails up to an inch long that become most evident on a rising tide as they climb the stems of the marsh grass. These hard-shelled snails feed on organic matter accumulated on the stems of the vegetation.

A faint trail leads across a 100-yard stretch of dunes to the windward beach. Use insect repellent here, or make the trip at a fast trot. Fortunately, the mosquitoes rarely venture out onto the beach, so you will have a safe haven when you reach the shores of Tangier Sound. Unfortunately, here you face different kinds of winged terrors. By late summer, deerflies, green-heads, and an ankle-biting relative of the housefly patrol the beach. Because of the prevailing breezes, however, they stay low and typically alight only on immobile sunbathers. For this reason, active beachcombing rather than passive tanning is the recommended pastime out here. If all this sounds unpleasant, it's really not; the beach is actually an enjoyable place.

Northward, the beach stretches for only a short distance, about a third of a mile. At Rock Hole, several tidal guts connect Tangier Sound with the interior of Janes Island. It is possible to wade or swim across these narrow channels to gain access to the more remote beach near Flatcap Point.

To the south, the beach runs for several miles to the southern terminus of the island at Old House Cove. This is prime Chesapeake

country, and it gives the impression that if you're not at the end of the world, you can at least see it from here. Tangier Sound is located at the widest part of the Bay, and no land is visible for a full 180-degree sweep. Behind you are the seemingly endless marshes of the lower Chesapeake Bay. Only the condos of Crisfield, far to the southeast, disturb the horizon.

The beach on the island is rather narrow, perhaps 25 feet wide in most places. Windrows of eelgrass, dislodged from the Bay bottom by storms, pile up on the beach. The hand of humans is clearly visible as well, despite the feeling of solitude. Trash, especially plastic items, lies half buried in sand or decorates the shrubbery that backs the forebeach. Such detritus, which nature cannot decompose, is unfortunate but not unexpected; studies of the most remote islands in the world show similar kinds of human flotsam.

Walk as far as you like and then return to your canoe or kayak. You may paddle back to the mainland by the same route; paddling distance is only about a mile. However, energetic paddlers may explore as many of the saltwater guts dissecting Janes Island as they choose to in order to extend the trip. The park service has created three other water trails, marked by color-coded signs, that wind through the marshes in convoluted routes (a good map helps with route finding). The scenery is similar on each of these passages, but all are pleasant, and there is always the mystery of what might be around the next bend. It is also possible to gain access to Tangier Sound from the beach dock by paddling northward and staying left at all forks (the green trail). Within less than a mile, this route brings you out at Rock Hole. Circumnavigation of Janes Island is possible, but it is a twelve-mile trip over exposed water, where tides and wind can make for slow going.

Directions

From Baltimore or Washington, DC, take Route 50 over the Bay Bridge to Salisbury. After passing through the business district, take Route 13 south. Exit Route 13 onto Route 413, following the signs for Crisfield. Once the highway becomes separated by a grassy median in "suburban" Crisfield, look for the brown Janes Island State Park sign. Turn right at this sign onto Route 358 and go 1.5 miles to the park entrance.

Other Outdoor Recreational Opportunities Nearby

From Crisfield, it's possible to take the ferry to Smith Island for a day trip or overnight visit (make reservations for accommodations in advance). Smith Island is a unique cultural experience, and nature is always close at hand. Assateague Island is about a half-hour's drive from Janes Island, and has hiking, cycling, and paddling options.

BLUE CRABS

If there is any one animal that embodies the essence of Maryland, it is undoubtedly the blue crab. Inhabiting Chesapeake Bay in a plentitude that recalls the historic bounty of our great estuary, blue crabs play an important role in the ecology and economy of the Bay. The crab fishery is by far the most important one in the Chesapeake, and more people eat more crabs here in Maryland than anywhere else. A truly democratic cuisine, crabs are enjoyed by everyone, from the richest blueblood in Potomac or Green-spring Valley to the poorest chicken-necker in Baltimore or Cris-field. Even the Latin scientific name, *Callinectes sapidus*, says it all: *callinectes* means "beautiful swimmer," and *sapidus* means "tasty" or "savory." Yet there is much that we do not know about blue crabs and their management and conservation, so we cannot be certain that our grandchildren will enjoy these tasty crustaceans in the abundance we do today.

Blue crabs mate in mid-Bay, mostly in early summer. Females then move down the Bay into the high-salinity waters of Virginia, where the eggs are extruded. The yellowish orange egg mass clings to the underside of the female, and after several weeks the eggs hatch to release the earliest larval form, the zoeae. These pinhead-sized planktonic larvae are at the mercy of currents and tides, and they are often swept out into the Atlantic Ocean. Survivors eventually molt into the next larval stage, called the megalops, which look like tiny lobsters. Megalops sink to the bottom, where the heavier, saltier water generally trends back into the Bay, carrying them along. The success of any year's spawn depends in great measure on these poorly understood life history stages and the factors that control their movements. After a few more molts, tiny crabs emerge, growing slowly as they feed in the sheltered waters of eelgrass beds and shallows.

After 12 to 16 months of precarious existence, blue crabs reach sexual maturity. Crabs are easily sexed by the shape of the apron, or the abdomen, on the underside. Males have a "Washington Monument" shell section bisecting the apron whereas females have a more rounded "Capitol Dome." The tips of the largest claws are red in females. Crabs typically live for two years, rarely three. Winters are spent torpid, buried in mud in deep parts of the Bay.

Each winter since 1990, the blue crab population in Chesapeake Bay has been sampled by the "winter dredge survey." This scientific study visits 1,500 sites Bay-wide in water deeper than five feet between December and March. A six-foot wide dredge is towed through the muddy bottom of the Bay for one minute at a speed of three knots. The dredge is then hauled aboard and all crabs are counted, measured, and sexed.

(continued)

In 2016, there were 553 million crabs in the Bay, according to this survey. The blue crab population of Chesapeake Bay is quite variable, as might be expected for a short-lived animal influenced by physical factors like weather and biological factors like predators (including humans) and competitors. The blue crab population of the Bay was about twice as high in the years 1990–1997 as in 1998–2009; since then, the numbers have been more variable but with a general upward trend that has permitted a sustainable harvest. However, in 2011 a target number for spawning-age females was established at 215 million; that number has been reached only twice since 1990. Managers at Maryland's Department of Natural Resources, advised by scientists, make decisions annually about harvests, adjusting the length of the crabbing season, size limits, and catch limits for both commercial and recreational crabbers.

While regulations regarding crabbing are always controversial among the various competing stakeholders, the blue crab fishery has a few things in its favor. The crab population has never crashed to levels that make recovery difficult, no diseases plague blue crabs, and water quality issues rarely affect the motile and adaptable crustacean. The dredge surveys are scientifically accurate, permit precise comparisons year to year, and are not controversial. The public at large generally trusts management decisions regarding the blue crab, due to a successful past track record. As long as savory steamed Chesapeake Bay blue crabs grace newspaper-covered tables on hot summer evenings, Marylanders will always rejoice in this one part of the natural bounty comprising "The Land of Pleasant Living."

Pocomoke River

River Section: Porters Crossing to Snow Hill
County: Worcester
Distance: 5.1 miles
Difficulty: Easy, except when windy. Tidal flatwater
Hazards: Gusty winds possible in lower half
Tide Information: https://tidesandcurrents.noaa.gov/tide_predictions.html;
    select Maryland and scroll to the Snow Hill station
Highlights: A beautiful bald cypress swamp that changes from narrow and
    intimate to open with expansive views in just a five-mile paddling trip
Nearby Canoe/Kayak Rental: Pocomoke River Canoe Company,
    www.pocomokerivercanoe.com, (410) 632-3971
More Information: Pocomoke River State Park, http://dnr.maryland.gov
    /Publiclands/Pages/eastern/pocomokeriver.aspx, (410) 632-2566
Street Address: None available (Porters Crossing put-in); 2 River Street,
    Snow Hill, Maryland 21863 (take-out)
GPS Coordinates: 38.222817, 75363287 (Porters Crossing put-in);
    38.178848, 75.394111 (Snow Hill take-out)

What's the best canoe trip in Maryland? Paddlers will debate this topic endlessly, but one river keeps coming up on everyone's list: the Pocomoke. This small river on the lower Eastern Shore has it all: great scenery, frequent glimpses of wildlife, and a remote, intimate quality difficult to find in a state as populous as Maryland. The logistics of a canoe or kayak trip on the Pocomoke are simple, too. The five-mile run from Porters Crossing to Snow Hill is just the right length for an easy day on the river. There's a friendly and informative outfitter right at the take-out for those who need to rent a canoe or obtain a car shuttle. Campsites are available nearby in one of the prettiest state park campgrounds in Maryland. Yet despite all these attributes, you'll be unlikely to see any other paddlers on the river.

The Pocomoke River drains a large, shallow basin occupying the central part of the lower Eastern Shore. Much of it is low-lying swamp, dense and impenetrable, seemingly composed of equal parts water, mud, and tangled vegetation. Although the fringes of the drainage basin have been converted into farmland, much of the heart of the Pocomoke is still wild and remote. It is the most northerly of the southern hardwood swamps, harboring a number of plants and animals more typical of river systems far to the south. At least eighteen species of warblers nest here, and there are more kinds of breeding birds than on any similarly sized tract in the mid-Atlantic states. Birders from all over Maryland gather in the spring to look and listen for Swainson's warbler, an elusive and rare songster more typical of North Carolina and points south. Among the mammals, you may spot the shy and reclusive river otter. In recognition of the ecological significance of the swamp, the Nature Conservancy has purchased almost 15,000 acres, some of which have been conveyed to the state.

The Pocomoke is a special place in every season. Situated in the warmest region in Maryland, the river is frozen only rarely, and it is a good choice for a winter cruise. Long vistas open up across the swamps, revealing the bare trunks of trees that are hidden at other seasons. For the competent and well-prepared canoeist or kayaker, the rewards of wintertime paddling are many. Spring comes slowly to the swamps, but when the trees leaf out, wildlife activity becomes frantic. By midsummer, animal action has slowed, languishing in the heat, but the heavily shaded river corridor is still a refuge from high temperatures. Finally, fall brings the color of autumn leaves drifting over the river in a reminder that the cycle of seasons is nearing its end.

Trip Description

Porters Crossing, a wooden bridge across the Pocomoke, marks the start of this paddling trip. It's deep in a damp, shady wetland forest where birdsong abounds and the temperature on a hot summer day is ten degrees cooler than in the surrounding agricultural fields. There is plenty of roadside parking, and a dry, sandy slope leads down to the water for an easy put-in.

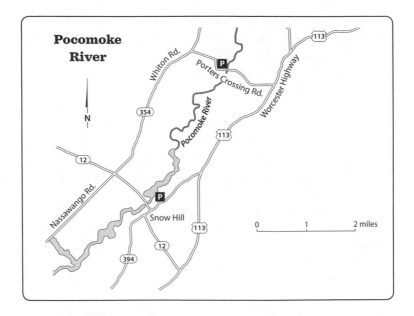

The first mile of the Pocomoke is narrow; trees span the width of the river overhead. These woods are known as bald cypress swamps, for their dominant tree species. Bald cypress trees, although not the most numerous species, are the largest in the swamp, with a stringy bark, feathery short needles, and an exotic, southern appearance. The most noteworthy feature of these trees is their "knees," aptly named protuberances that surround the trunk. Scientists are still uncertain about the function of cypress knees. Some believe that they provide a way for tree roots to exchange oxygen with the atmosphere, since the muddy soils of swamps tend to be rather anaerobic. Other scientists feel that the whole network of knees provides support, much like the pontoons on an outrigger canoe. Some knees may be found at quite a distance from the tree, and several have been discovered lurking just under the surface of the water in the main channel. If you should ride up on a cypress knee or other log, just relax, try to keep your weight in the center of the boat, and work your way off the obstacle with gentle shoves.

In late spring, this first mile of the Pocomoke may be the best place in Maryland to see the spectacular prothonotary warbler. Breeding territories are laid out along the river banks in a serried row, spaced about every hundred yards. Within each territory, the

male sings loudly from a perch and forages for insects in a conspicuous fashion in the overhead branches and along the tree trunks and
brush piles along the banks. Chases between birds are common at the
edges of territories. Although prothonotaries are diminutive, their
bright golden color and active lifestyle make them endearing.

This first mile of river is narrow and there are sometimes downed
tree trunks in the water or leaning over the passage at head height.
There is always a cleared route, however, as long as you align your
boat for the opening in advance. Avoid any vines that might drape
leaning trees; many are poison ivy, an exceedingly common plant
in this swamp. Look for leaflets in groups of three, or small, white
berries, or hairy stems, all of which are characteristic of this dermatologic nightmare. But not every vine is poison ivy; crossvine is a
rare plant found in Maryland only in the Pocomoke drainage basin.
It has beautiful yellow and orange tubular flowers in late spring and
a lovely scent.

Most people associate swamps with biting insects, but insects are rarely a problem along the Pocomoke, especially if you stay on the water. Gnats and mosquitoes may be plentiful after a rain in late spring and summer, however, especially if you leave your canoe or kayak. If it looks like insects are going to be a problem on shore, eat lunch in the boats, tying them up to a tree so you don't drift downriver.

The water in the Pocomoke is clear and clean, unless there has been a recent rain. It is, however, stained the color of tea from tannins leaching out of the surrounding swamp. Where the bottom is sandy, the colors combine to give an orange cast to the water.

After about a mile of this prime swamp cruising, you will emerge into a gradually widening Pocomoke where tree branches no longer span the river. The increased sunlight permits the growth of spatterdock in shallow, muddy areas. Spatterdock has large, flat green leaves that form a mat on the water that in turn hosts spiders and insects.

Your only opportunity to get out of your boat, stretch your legs, or enjoy a snack is encountered exactly halfway through the trip. Look for a set of powerlines that span the river; another hundred yards brings you to a hillside with easy access from the river.

Just beyond this point, the Pocomoke widens yet again, and it is a few hundred yards wide most of the rest of the way to Snow Hill. Even so, there is no development, and only one house, visible from the water. The Pocomoke is a beautiful and enchanting spot, a slice of the timelessness that infuses such special places. Take out on the left-hand side of the river at a bulkhead forming the lower end of a municipal parking lot, just before the Route 12 bridge in Snow Hill. The Pocomoke River Canoe Company is located here, and it has canoe and kayak rentals available.

Directions

From Baltimore or Washington, DC, cross the Bay Bridge and continue south on Route 50 to Salisbury. Exit onto Route 13 south, the Salisbury bypass. Turn left on Route 12 and continue to the town of Snow Hill. Cross the bridge over the Pocomoke and make your first left turn into an alley next to the Pocomoke River Canoe Company. A municipal parking lot is directly ahead of you. There are no public facilities here.

To reach the river access point at Porters Crossing, begin from the same parking lot. Take Route 12 north, crossing the Pocomoke and leaving Snow Hill. At the first major intersection, a blinking light, turn right on Route 354. Porters Crossing Road is on your right 3.4 miles up this road.

Other Outdoor Recreational Opportunities Nearby

For paddlers, Nassawango Creek, Dividing Creek, and Corkers Creek are located just a few miles away. Bicycling trails at Assateague Island National Seashore and at Chincoteague National Wildlife Refuge are each about a 45-minute drive from the Snow Hill area. There are some pleasant, short walking trails at Pocomoke River State Park (Shad Landing area) and at Furnace Town, both located less than a 20-minute drive from Snow Hill.

PROTHONOTARY WARBLERS

Of all the animals that are found in wooded swamps like those along the Pocomoke River, perhaps none is more characteristic than the prothonotary warbler. Noisy, active, relatively unafraid of people, and outfitted in a spectacular plumage, the prothonotary endears itself to everyone who canoes or kayaks here. Named for a brightly robed official of the Vatican, prothonotaries virtually define wooded swamps on Maryland's Coastal Plain.

Prothonotaries are fairly large as warblers go, reaching almost the size of a bluebird. Their entire head and chest are a golden yellow that may range almost to orange. Their wings are blue-gray, and their backs have an olive shading. Females are similar to males in plumage, although they may be a bit duller.

The prothonotary is the only eastern warbler that nests in a cavity, typically a hole excavated by a woodpecker in a dead tree. For this reason, the young are protected against such predators as crows, blue jays, and raccoons. However, because they use what are essentially "recycled" nest sites, mites, fleas, and other parasites may take a heavier toll on nestlings than is typical for other warblers. In addition, nest sites may be hard to find; other species such as tree swallows, wrens, starlings, and house sparrows all begin nesting before prothonotaries and thus claim the best sites. Upon their arrival in the swamps in late April, prothonotaries spend the majority of their time searching and inspecting prospective nesting sites. Once a nest is built, the male is quite territorial, aggressively driving off all intruders, whether of the same or of different species.

Cowbird predation can be a problem for prothonotaries; one nest was found containing seven cowbird eggs and no warbler eggs. The farther the nest site is from agricultural fields, scrub, and other disturbed habitats, the less parasitism is likely to occur. For this reason, reproductive success is usually greater in unbroken tracts of swamp forest.

Prothonotaries typically lay four to six small eggs in a lined nest. After a 12- to 14-day incubation period, immobile, blind, naked young hatch. They develop quickly and fledge within 11 days; the young are capable of swimming, an important ability since nest sites are frequently over water.

Prothonotary warblers begin migrating in late summer, wintering in Central America, northern South America, and the Antilles. We like to think of prothonotaries and other migrants as "our" birds, but in fact they spend more than half the year elsewhere. For this reason, the conservation of migratory birds depends on proper conditions and habitat in three places: the summer breeding grounds, the wintering grounds, and stopover places visited during migration. Despite these complexities—as well as the problems caused by deforestation, cowbird parasitism, and competition for nesting sites—prothonotaries are one of the few species of warblers that seem to be holding their own. For Maryland naturalists, that's good news, because there are few animals more colorful in plumage and more charming in behavior than prothonotaries.

Corkers Creek

River Section: Shad Landing marina upstream to head of navigation
  and return
County: Worcester
Distance: About 2 miles round trip
Difficulty: Easy. Tidal flatwater
Hazards: None
Tide Information: https://tidesandcurrents.noaa.gov/tide_predictions.html;
  select Maryland and scroll to the Snow Hill station
Highlights: A narrow and intimate bald cypress swamp notable for wildlife
  sightings
Nearby Canoe/Kayak Rental: Pocomoke River State Park, Shad Landing
  area, (410) 632-2566
More Information: Pocomoke River State Park, Shad Landing area,
  http://dnr.maryland.gov/publiclands/Pages/eastern/pocomokeriver.aspx,
  (410) 632-2566
Street Address: 3461 Worcester Highway, Snow Hill, Maryland 21863
GPS Coordinates: 38.139828, 75.441109 (marina)

Corkers Creek is a narrow tidal stream on which the Shad Landing area of Pocomoke River State Park is located. Corkers has many assets to recommend itself: it is scenic, it is wild, and it is convenient to the campsites at Shad Landing. On top of that, it is short, for those with limited time or active children, and kayaks and canoes can be rented at the Shad Landing marina. For these reasons, it's probably the most frequently paddled river on the Eastern Shore. Even so, it is remarkable how a sense of wildness pervades the creek and its banks as soon as that flotilla of Boy Scouts disappears around the next bend.

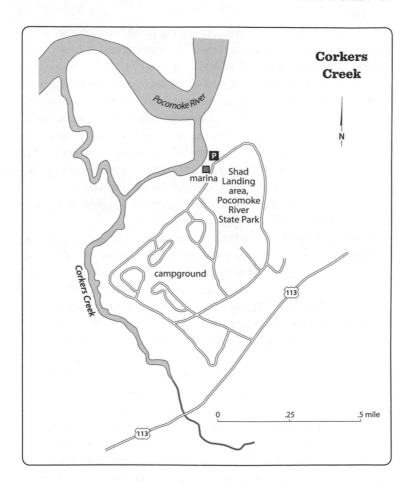

Trip Description

Begin (and end) your trip at the Shad Landing marina of Pocomoke River State Park. There's plenty of parking, as well as wheelchair-accessible bathrooms, water, trash cans, and a camp store (with wonderful, cheap ice cream cones!). It's also a great place to camp, perhaps the best in Maryland; the wind whispers in the tops of 100-foot-tall loblolly pines shading the campsites, and in summer there's a pool for the kids.

Dodge the power boats and fishing lines as you paddle out of the marina into the creek. Although Corkers is tidal, the range is not great, so it's easy to paddle against the current.

Immediately opposite the marina on the far shore are some semi-submerged logs and tiny hammocks of vegetation, and it is here that you'll have a fine chance to observe sunning turtles. Despite the heavy river traffic, they usually frequent this spot. The turtles you see here are most likely to be painted turtles. The painted turtle has the widest range, and is perhaps the most common, of any turtle in North America. It has yellow, orange, or reddish stripes on its neck, legs, and tail, and similar colors typically show at the edges of the plates forming the shell. The smallest turtles in a group seem to be the most skittish and will usually dive first as you approach, whereas the larger ones seem the most loathe to move. Adult painted turtles are herbivorous.

Paddle upriver (to the left as you leave the marina; sometimes it's hard to tell on a tidal creek). This section of Corkers was dredged years ago to provide access to the marina; you can tell by the arrow-straight nature of the river channel and the now well-forested spoil banks on the left shore. The branches of riverside shrubs and small trees hang far over the water in their search for sunlight, and many are decorated with plastic bobbers from errant casts by fishermen.

After about 200 yards, the canal enters the true Corkers Creek. Head to the left (upstream); the right branch will take you out to the Pocomoke River. You now enter a natural wooded swamp. Although there are trees and vegetation along the banks, a close examination of the ground will reveal that the soil is as much water as solid earth. About the only firm footing is around the little hammocks of vegetation growing at the base of a root or tree stump. For this reason, it's difficult to get back into an overturned boat, so do your best to stay upright.

The natural river here winds back and forth in broad, sweeping turns. The channel is usually deepest on the outside of a turn, whereas mudflats build up on the inside as particulates fall out of the more slowly moving water. As a result, rivers tend to meander, forming ever-widening, snakelike bends. During floods, these turns buffer the shores from the erosive effects of water by slowing the current. Inexplicably, the Soil Conservation Service has spent hundreds of millions of dollars to channelize and straighten small creeks and streams. The result is the loss of soil, not its conservation.

Emergent vegetation populates the muddy shallows. The most common plant is spatterdock, a round, tropical-looking leaf that appears to float on the water's surface at high tide. Its yellow, lotus-like flower prompts many people erroneously to call it a water lily. Summertime paddlers may also notice a blue spike of flowers from a plant with arrow-shaped leaves; this is pickerelweed.

Many kinds of trees line the shore. Oak, ash, alder, sweet gum, and red maple are common. But it is the unusual trees that are most interesting. Three species grow here on Corkers Creek that are on the northern edge of their distribution: the fringe tree, the sweetbay magnolia, and the bald cypress. The fringe tree flowers in May, and its white, ribbonlike petals (from which it gets its common name) make it unmistakable. In June, the sweetbay magnolia unfolds its large, fragrant blossoms. But it is the bald cypress that is the dominant tree in this swamp. The high water table in the swamp keeps most tree species under 40 feet in height, but this uniform canopy is punctuated by the occasional very tall bald cypress. Unusual as a deciduous conifer, it has feathery needles that are lime green in early spring and rusty reddish brown in fall. Outcroppings of its root structure, aptly named "knees," form little islands of soil and herbaceous vegetation around the base of the big trees.

Corkers Creek is a great place to see birds, especially in the early morning and again at dusk. You're likely to see great blue herons, green-backed herons, various woodpeckers, mallards, kingbirds, and other less easily identifiable forest-dwelling birds. Look for turkey vultures soaring high overhead, accompanied on occasion by the scream of a soaring red-tailed hawk. The "who-cooks-for-you" call of a barred owl is also common.

In spring and summer, you'll undoubtedly see prothonotary warblers. These engaging denizens of wooded swamps have bright yellow chests and heads and blue-gray wings. They're completely oblivious to humans; I've been so close as to feel the brush of air from their wingbeats and I have seen them glean a branch for insects within a paddle length of my head.

As the creek winds toward its source, it narrows considerably until it is overhung by trees. Water snakes drape themselves on these branches on hot summer days, and park naturalists enjoy spinning partly true tales of these tubular reptiles dropping into the boats of unsuspecting paddlers. Since water snakes can be pugnacious, it's best to keep your eyes open and not interrupt their reptilian siestas. The poisonous cottonmouth, or water moccasin, is not found in

Maryland, despite the wide-eyed attestations of many paddlers on Corkers Creek.

Soon after narrowing to only a canoe width, Corkers Creek passes under Route 113. On the far side, trees temporarily recede from the river banks, leaving a nice freshwater marsh. Here you can find vegetation of a type not heretofore seen on the trip: cattails, blue irises, jewelweeds, tearthumbs, and smartweeds. Lacing many of these herbaceous marsh plants together is dodder, an orange-stemmed vine twining through the vegetation. It has no true roots but gains nourishment from the vascular systems of the plants on which it grows. A few old wildflower texts refer to dodder as mother-in-law plant. Why? Because it is parasitic and the stem resembles a long, red, wagging tongue!

Continue upriver, poling your way through the shallows and parting the vegetation with your paddle. The stream will be only a bit wider than your boat here, and at all but the highest tide you may have to retreat. But at high tide, you can reach an enchanting forest dell of bald cypress that Dr. Charles Stine of Johns Hopkins University calls the Hobbitt's Glen. It is cool and shady, with only the occasional shaft of sunlight penetrating to your boat. Moss and ferns abound; cypress knees poke up everywhere. This is the end of the line, even at high tide, so back your way out to a point where the kayak or canoe can be turned around.

Go back to Shad Landing by the same route. The turn that leads to the marina is marked by a sign. Keep an eye peeled for birds and turtles on the return trip, as they tend to resume their riverside haunts rather quickly after disturbance. The total distance of this paddle is only about two miles; allot two to three hours for the moderate pace needed to poke about, admire your surroundings, and really enjoy the scenery and wildlife.

Directions

From Baltimore or Washington, DC, cross the Bay Bridge and continue south on Route 50 to Salisbury. Exit onto Route 13 south, the Salisbury bypass. Turn left on Route 12 through the town of Snow Hill. Turn right onto Route 113. The Shad Landing area of the Pocomoke River State Park is found on Route 113 about two miles south of the southern "suburbs" of Snow Hill. Once in the park, follow signs to the marina. An admission fee is charged.

Other Outdoor Recreational Opportunities Nearby

Nassawango Creek and the Pocomoke River, located within a 15-minute drive, are both superb paddling streams. Hiking is possible on the Paul Leifer Trail, located within a 15-minute drive, and on Assateague Island National Seashore. Paved bike trails are available on Assateague Island National Seashore and at Chincoteague National Wildlife Refuge, both about 45 minutes away by car.

WHAT'S IN A (LATIN) NAME?

Many people who read articles in the popular press about plants and animals are confused about scientists' curious insistence on calling organisms by a Latin name. For example, we humans are called *Homo sapiens*. Why this strange practice, in a dead language?

The answer is both practical and historic. In practical terms, common names are sometimes ambiguous. For example, birds called "robins" are found in both North America and Great Britain, but American and British robins are remarkably different birds. Similarly, a single species can be known by multiple common names. For example, *Houstonia caerulea* is variously called bluets, innocence, and Quaker ladies.

Every kind of organism known to science has been given its own unique Latin name. It consists of two names, the genus and the species. These words usually reflect some aspect of the organism's structure, use, or discovery. For example, *homo* is Latin for "man," while *sapiens* means "having sense."

Latin binomials are given to a newly discovered organism by the scientist who first publishes a valid description of it in a scientific journal. Many common species were named in the eighteenth century by Carolus Linnaeus, who first used this system to classify organisms on the basis of similar morphologies. Linnaeus chose Latin not only because it was the language of educated people at that time, but to ensure that there could be no confusion about how a name would translate from one language to another.

(continued)

The etymology of these Latin names is frequently obscure but almost always fascinating. Here are a few examples of genus names given to wildflowers:

Achillea: the common garden plant and wildflower yarrow was named for the Greek hero Achilles. According to legend, Achilles carried this plant with him to war, using it to staunch the flow of blood from wounds.

Panax: the well-known herb ginseng. Its Latin name is derived from two Greek words, *pan*, meaning "all," and *akos*, meaning "cure." Hence, ginseng is literally a panacea, a cure-all, reflecting the great value some societies place on its root as a tonic and aphrodisiac.

Sanguinaria: the beautiful white spring wildflower whose common name is bloodroot. The Latin word *sanguis* means "blood." The reference is to the red rootstock, which exudes an orangish liquid.

Aquilegia: another equally beautiful spring wildflower, columbine. The genus name is derived from the Latin for "eagle" and refers to the resemblance between the five spurs and an eagle's claw.

Helianthus: this plant has the closest possible correlation between its Latin genus and its English common name, sunflower. It comes from the Greek words *helios*, meaning "sun," and *anthos*, meaning "flower."

Tussilago: one of our earliest spring wildflowers, coltsfoot, looks like a dandelion and grows in the disturbed soil along roadsides. *Tussilago* means "cough dispeller"; an extract was used in colonial American cough medicines.

These are just a few of the Latin names of common wildflowers. Many of the references are much more obscure, but their investigation is always a fascinating and rewarding endeavor.

Dividing Creek

River Section: Winter Quarters Landing to Dividing Creek to head of
navigation and return
Counties: Somerset, Worcester
Distance: 3 miles one way to Dividing Creek Road
Difficulty: Easy. Tidal flatwater
Hazards: None
Tide Information: https://tidesandcurrents.noaa.gov/tide_predictions.html;
select Maryland and scroll to the Snow Hill station
Highlights: A remote and lightly paddled freshwater swamp run
Nearby Canoe/Kayak Rental: Pocomoke River Canoe Company,
www.pocomokerivercanoe.com, (410) 632-3971
More Information: Pocomoke River Canoe Company, (410) 632-3971
Street Address: 399 Winter Quarters Drive, Pocomoke City, Maryland 21851
(Winter Quarters boat ramp)
GPS Coordinates: 38.085770, 75.559312 (Winter Quarters boat ramp)

The Pocomoke River watershed on Maryland's lower eastern
shore is a paddler's paradise, featuring at least four stream segments, each suitable for a wonderful day of canoeing or kayaking, and
all within a 20-minute drive of one another. Each is narrow, allowing
close views of wildlife, and every one is scenic, different enough from
most of Maryland that it seems just a little bit exotic. Despite the
similarities, Corker's, Nassawango, Pocomoke, and Dividing have
unique subtleties. Dividing Creek, in particular, is singular because
it maintains its narrow, intimate character for so much of its length.
You'll likely run out of strength and the desire to paddle before you
run out of river.

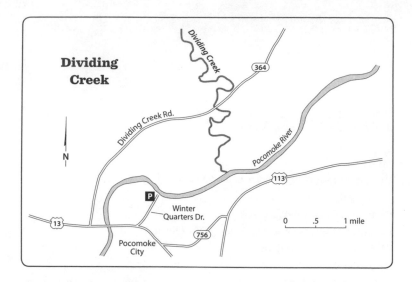

Trip Description

Begin your paddling trip from Winter Quarters Landing just outside of Pocomoke City. There is parking for a half dozen cars, trash cans, and a boat ramp, but no other facilities. Launch and paddle upstream (to your right as you face the water). Cross the river and then stay near the far shore; some sizeable barges travel the Pocomoke from time to time. The Pocomoke has the reputation of being surprisingly deep for its narrow width, permitting large boats to motor upstream as far as Snow Hill.

As you leave Winter Quarters Landing behind, little evidence of human activity is visible. Big trees, especially bald cypress, line the shore, which is thick and seemingly impenetrable with vegetation. Fall color is good along the Pocomoke, as red maple is a common tree that is capable of growing in the wet soil of the river's edge. After a mile of paddling, look for an opening in the trees to your left. Dividing Creek is no more than thirty feet wide, even here at its mouth.

Dividing Creek winds through all points of the compass in the almost two miles between its mouth and the bridge at Dividing Creek Road. There are surprisingly few trees blocking upstream progress. In part, this is because the trees growing close to the water are mostly small. Two common small trees are sweetbay magnolia and fringe tree. Both are less than twenty feet high, both are at the

northern edge of their natural range here in the Pocomoke watershed, and both have exceptionally beautiful flowers. Sweetbay magnolia flowers are the size of a cup, have creamy white petals, flaunt large pistils and stamens, and possess perhaps the most fragrant scent of any tree. Fringe tree sports hundreds of confetti-like petals that resemble exploding fireworks—no other tree has flowers in any way similar.

The wetland forest surrounding Dividing Creek, like the rest of the Pocomoke watershed, is characterized by bald cypress trees. These graceful, feathery forest giants tower over the other trees of the swamp. They thrive in wet, mucky soils, but prefer not to be totally inundated; in such watery conditions, trees tend to have swollen bases whose diameter at two feet above water level may be twice that at eight feet. These solitary bald cypress often support their own little island ecosystem of ferns, shrubs, and mosses at the base. Most bald cypress also have "knees," woody protuberances a foot or two in height and up to six inches in diameter that surround the trunk like a worshipful assembly of little forest gnomes. These knees likely help support the main trunk and may also function in gas exchange, given the anoxic soils of the swamp.

Paddling up a river such as Dividing Creek seems like a journey through the forest primeval, but actually humans have exploited these cypress swamps for more than two centuries. Bald cypress wood is resistant to rot, and harvesting, especially for roofing and siding shingles, was a thriving industry for two centuries. Large tracts of cypress swamps in the Pocomoke watershed were essentially clearcut, permitting sunlight to dry the swamp, its low vegetation like sphagnum moss, and its peat substrate. Wildfires became common. One conflagration, in 1792, burned an estimated 3,000 acres in twelve hours. Another, in the 1930s, smoldered for eight months. What had been known as the Great Cypress Swamp became useless, abandoned land, and has been left all but undisturbed for the last eighty years. What you see from the seat of your canoe or kayak is the visible evidence of how nature can regenerate itself, given enough time and space.

The water in Dividing Creek, like that in many Coastal Plain rivers, is an orange color similar to that of tea. In large measure, this color is due to tannins, complex chemicals manufactured by plants that grow in acidic, nutrient-poor soils. Once thought to deter grazing by herbivores, tannins may also function in cellular metabolism, given their ability to bind proteins and their sequestration in special structures within the plant cell. As plants die, they release their water soluble tannins to the environment, staining the water in bogs, streams, and rivers. If this water is filtered to remove bacteria and other contaminants, it will be perfectly drinkable despite retaining its orange-brown hue.

About two miles from its confluence with the Pocomoke, Dividing Creek passes under Route 364, Dividing Creek Road, where a few houses are visible. It is not possible to take out here, as the surrounding land is all private. Continue paddling upstream as far as you care to or as far as fallen trees allow, then return by the same route.

Directions

From Washington, DC, or Baltimore, cross the Chesapeake Bay Bridge and continue south on Route 50 through Easton, Cambridge, and Salisbury. In Salisbury, take the bypass, Route 13, south for about 25 miles. Cross the bridge over the Pocomoke River and make your first left onto Winter Quarters Drive. Go to the end.

Other Outdoor Recreational Opportunities Nearby

Excellent paddling trips may be enjoyed on the Pocomoke River, Nassawango Creek, Corkers Creek, and at Janes Island State Park, all within a 30-minute drive and described elsewhere in this book.

WHAT IS BIODIVERSITY?

There are few concepts in science today more fashionable—and more misunderstood—than biological diversity. Everyone is for biological diversity; like Mom, apple pie, rain forests, and whales, it is a modern cause célèbre. Yet most people have only a hazy understanding of what biological diversity (usually referred to as biodiversity) really is. Even among scientists there is sometimes disagreement.

One of the simplest yet most complete definitions of biodiversity is "the variety and variability among living organisms and the ecological complexes in which they occur." This definition implies that there are at least three components of biodiversity: variety of ecological communities within an ecosystem, numbers of species, and genetic variation among individuals.

Community diversity is perhaps the easiest to understand. It is merely the variety of habitats found within an ecosystem. For example, a barrier island ecosystem like Assateague Island contains several habitats: intertidal zone, beach, dunes, shrub zone, maritime forest, salt marsh, and freshwater pools. Different kinds of plants and animals live in each habitat. The more habitat types there are, the greater is the area's community diversity.

(continued)

A second component of biodiversity is species diversity. This refers to the number of species present within a habitat. For example, the species diversity of a cornfield is rather low; there is only one plant species present (corn), and for this reason the number of species of insects, fungi, soil bacteria, birds, and small mammals is correspondingly low. By comparison, a similarly sized plot of abandoned farmland has a diverse collection of organisms. It will contain more species of every one of these groups of organisms, and it therefore harbors greater species diversity.

The most difficult component of biodiversity to understand is genetic diversity. This term applies to the variety of information coded for in the genes of different members of any one species. For example, wolves were once widely distributed throughout North America. Certain races or subspecies of wolves were specifically adapted to particular habitats; those found in the southern swamps were remarkably different from those of the northern tundra, in both physical appearance and behavior. Although these two races of wolves could interbreed, their individual genetic makeups were different enough that any blurring of them would impoverish the gene pool that serves as the basis for future natural selection and evolution. We have no idea what traits will be important for the future survival of a species, so conservation biology advises us to preserve all of the raw materials upon which natural selection acts. As Aldo Leopold said, "To keep every cog and wheel is the first precaution of intelligent tinkering."

Preservation of biodiversity therefore consists of more than merely saving rare or endangered species. On the largest scale, it encompasses preservation of landscapes and the habitats they contain. It applies to both rare and common species, valuing neither one over the other. And it implies that subtle genetic differences within a species over its entire geographic range have importance for evolution and should therefore be conserved. These principles are not trivial; they represent a paradigm shift in the way we look at and live with the natural world.

Nassawango Creek

River Section: Red House Road to Nassawango Road
County: Worcester
Distance: 2.3 miles one way
Difficulty: Easy. Tidal flatwater
Hazards: None
Tide Information: https://tidesandcurrents.noaa.gov/tide_predictions.html;
　select Maryland and scroll to the Snow Hill station
Highlights: A lovely intimate woodland stream whose waters emerge into an
　open freshwater marsh
Nearby Canoe/Kayak Rental: Pocomoke River Canoe Company,
　www.pocomokerivercanoe.com, (410) 632-3971
More Information: The Nature Conservancy (Maryland Field Office),
　www.nature.org/ourinitiatives/regions/northamerica/unitedstates
　/maryland_dc/index, (301) 897-8570
Street Address: Near 4108 Red House Road (launch point);
　near 4733 Nassawango Road (take-out)
GPS Coordinates: 38.189179, 75.454289 (Red House Road launch point);
　38.168348, 75.433669 (Nassawango Road take-out)

The Pocomoke River drainage basin on Maryland's lower Eastern
Shore abounds with superb paddling streams. Corkers Creek,
Dividing Creek, and the upper reaches of the Pocomoke itself are
all wild, intimate little aquatic gems. In large measure, this bounty
is due to unusually high depth-to-width ratios that lead to narrow
but passable watercourses. The geological origin of this characteristic is uncertain, but the result is certainly fortunate for paddlers.
Nassawango Creek, still another of the Pocomoke's tributaries, is no
exception to the rule.

Nassawango is one of Maryland's more unusual place names, and like many others, it is Native American in origin, meaning "ground between the streams." However, one old colonial map names the waterway as Askimenokonson Creek, from the Algonquian phrase "stony place where they pick early strawberries." What an idyllic name it is.

The Nassawango is the largest sub-basin in the Pocomoke drainage, and almost 10,000 acres of the swampy land has been bought by the Nature Conservancy for preservation. Renowned for its unique ecological character, Nassawango Creek is home to several species of plants and animals that are rare in Maryland or at the northernmost extension of their ranges. A canoe or kayak trip down the Nassawango is guaranteed to be a day filled with wildlife and scenery.

Trip Description

The put-in for Nassawango Creek is the river crossing at Red House Road, where there is roadside parking for perhaps a dozen cars. Red House Road marks the head of navigable waters; just upstream, the creek dissolves into a braid of shallow, vine-choked passages frequently blocked by downed trees. Red House Road is also the head of tidal action, so a long stretch of dry weather will have no effect on water level here. Many paddlers choose to do Nassawango Creek as an out-and-back trip, returning to Red House Road and thus requiring no car shuttle.

The river is only about 20 feet wide at the start, and it is overhung with trees that give the impression of paddling through a shady green tunnel. Red maple, river birch, sweet gum, green ash, and bald cypress form a diverse canopy. Closer to the ground, southern arrowwood, conspicuous by its clustered blue berries, hangs over the river. As its name implies, the shrub has long, straight twigs, which were used by Native Americans for arrow shafts.

Nassawango Creek hosts another tree species that was once common in Maryland but was all but extirpated. Atlantic white cedar grows in wet, swampy soil. Its wood is resistant to rot, so it was in demand for building purposes, and a few old structures still have original cedar shake shingles. In addition to being used for construction, Atlantic white cedar trees fell victim to the extensive timber harvesting required to make the charcoal used at the Nassawango

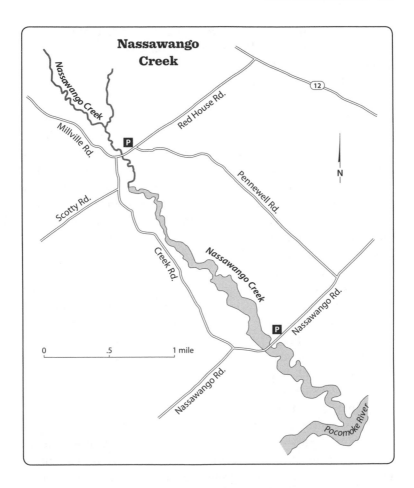

iron furnace. These white cedars are now rare, although the Nature Conservancy continues to plant seedlings in the swamps surrounding Nassawango Creek.

As with many small Coastal Plain streams, fallen trees may block progress downriver. Even if a passage has not been sawed out, smaller trees can frequently be bypassed or slipped under. Use care, however; poison ivy sometimes grows on such "strainers" as a hairy vine; it's wise to be able to recognize this dermatologic nemesis. Look for leaves in clusters of three: "leaflets three, let it be," as the saying goes. But another common vine is present on trees along Nassawango Creek, and it is worth a closer look. Crossvine is an unusual plant on the northernmost edge of its range. Flowering in late May, it has large, tubular orange flowers tipped with yellow at the edges. Crossvine takes its common name from the X-shaped pith revealed when the twig is cut in cross section.

Within a few hundred yards, Nassawango Creek widens enough for sunlight to penetrate to the river. A few clumps of spatterdock and pickerelweed begin to appear at the inside edges of bends where the river is shallow; these will form more extensive marshes in the creek's lower reaches. Patches of the rare and beautiful wild iris are also found. Sloughs branch out to either side, and this complex maze of water, marsh, and swamp almost always hides a few ducks (mallards or wood ducks) and wading birds like great blue herons, American egrets, and snowy egrets. Prothonotary warblers are also common in spring and summer, nesting in tree cavities and enlivening the creek with their distinctive songs. Indeed, this middle section where the river is neither too narrow nor too wide is the most likely place to surprise birds, sunning turtles, snakes, and insects, and even the occasional raccoon foraging for dinner. Overhead, raptors such as vultures, osprey, red-tailed hawks, and even bald eagles can often be seen soaring on thermals generated by the surrounding farmlands.

After many bends and about a mile and a half, Nassawango becomes wider still, and wind may become a factor on a blustery day. Many paddlers elect to return to Red House Road at this point, content in having visited the best of Nassawango Creek.

If you continue downstream, Nassawango Road is the recommended take-out, which of course requires a car shuttle. Limited parking is available along the road shoulders, which may be soft in wet weather. River distance from Red House Road to Nassawango Road is 2.3 miles. It is possible to continue paddling 1.0 mile to the confluence with the Pocomoke. At the junction, either turn left and proceed upstream for almost two miles to the Snow Hill City Park or turn right and proceed downstream for just over two miles to the Shad Landing area of Pocomoke River State Park. Note that the open nature of the Pocomoke and lower Nassawango may make for difficult paddling on windy days.

Directions

From Baltimore or Washington, DC, cross the Bay Bridge and continue south on Route 50 to Salisbury. Take the bypass, Route 13 (not

Business Route 13). Exit at Route 12. Continue south on Route 12 for about 15 miles, turning right onto Red House Road. The river crossing is one mile down this road.

Other Outdoor Recreational Opportunities Nearby

For paddlers, the Pocomoke River and Corkers Creek are located just a few miles away (these are described elsewhere in this book). Bicycling trails at Assateague Island National Seashore and at Chincoteague National Wildlife Refuge, in Virginia, are each about a 45-minute drive from the Snow Hill area. Just minutes away you can find a hiking trail through these same swamps at the Nature Conservancy's Nassawango Creek Preserve.

WHY PRESERVE BIODIVERSITY?

What is the importance of preserving biodiversity? Isn't it significant only for the tropics, where most of the earth's species are found? Why should you care?

Preserving biodiversity in Maryland is vital. At the most obvious, practical level, our natural resources are the basis of much commerce, including timber harvesting and the outdoor recreation industry. In addition, a majority of our medicines come from plant extracts, but most of our plants have never been surveyed for such beneficial compounds. On a more basic level, biodiversity has intrinsic importance to the quality of our lives, because even the most insulated city dweller is still dependent on our air, land, and water. It is safe to say that biodiversity contributes to the integrity, stability, and resilience of the planet's life support systems, and this is as true at the local and regional levels as it is at the global level. Finally, and perhaps most important, biological diversity is the raw material for evolution, a process that ensures adaptation to changing physical environments and the continuance of life on earth.

Biodiversity in Maryland is under constant attack. Unlike the tropics, where several species may go extinct each day because

(continued)

of human activity, here extinctions are not imminent. However, a great many populations of all sorts of organisms are being negatively affected and stressed by human dominance of the world. The biologist Paul Ehrlich likens this insidious loss of biodiversity to an airplane that loses a rivet here and a screw there. Each loss is insignificant by itself, but eventually the individual losses add up and the airplane falls apart. Loss of local biodiversity is a warning signal that our natural support systems are under stress and that they may fail at some point in the future, with uncertain consequences. The challenge for us is to stem that tide.

How can citizens preserve biological diversity in Maryland? In general, everything we can do to lessen our impact on the natural world will be helpful and in the long run beneficial to us as well. Health and prosperity decline in a deteriorating environment; we should endeavor to preserve our air, land, and water. In the past, approaches to conservation have been reactive, fixing things that are broken, rather than proactive. Thus we clean up pollution rather than reducing emissions from the pipe or smokestack; we institute growth management programs like the Critical Areas regulations in response to the degradation of Chesapeake Bay rather than managing growth before it gets out of hand; and we try to save endangered species instead of preserving the habitats and ecosystems of which they are a part. Our society needs to value our biological heritage just as we treasure our cultural heritage. Ultimately, we need to understand that the most significant evolutionary role we can play as the dominant species on earth today is that of an altruistic, careful, and conservative steward of our planet's riches, shepherding that natural heritage into an uncertain and unforeseeable future.

Blackwater National Wildlife Refuge

River Section: Section 1: Upper Blackwater River, Route 335 to footbridge
and return (green water trail)
Section 2: Coles Creek, Shorters Wharf to head of navigation and return
(orange water trail)
Section 3: Main Blackwater River, Shorters Wharf to Route 335
(purple water trail)

County: Dorchester

Distance: Section 1: 8 miles round trip, out and back
Section 2: 7.6 miles round trip, out and back
Section 3: 9 miles one way

Difficulty: Easy, except when windy. Tidal flatwater

Hazards: Wind, mud flats at low tide, hunting, biting insects

Tide Information: https://tidesandcurrents.noaa.gov/tide_predictions.html;
select Maryland and scroll to the McCready's Creek station

Highlights: Section 1: A scenic paddle to the headwaters of a freshwater
marsh in a national wildlife refuge renowned for its many migratory birds
Sections 2 and 3: Another scenic paddle into the remote heart of a national
wildlife refuge renowned for its migratory birds, but with a different
vegetation type (brackish marsh)

Nearby Kayak Rental: Blackwater Paddle and Pedal,
www.blackwaterpaddleandpedal.com, (410) 901-9255

More Information: Blackwater National Wildlife Refuge, www.fws.gov
/refuge/Blackwater, (410) 228-2677

Street Address: 2415 Key Wallace Drive, Cambridge, Maryland 21613
(Blackwater NWR Visitor Center); no street address available for
Shorters Wharf or the green trail put-in on Route 335)

GPS Coordinates: 38.444829, 76.119619 (Blackwater NWR Visitor Center); 38.439451, 76.145282 (green water trail put-in, Section 1); 38.381525, 76.067458 (Shorters Wharf, Sections 2 and 3)

B lackwater National Wildlife Refuge, near Cambridge, Maryland, is a place of great natural beauty, where sky and sea and land seem to merge into one diaphanous mélange pleasing to the eye and the spirit. There are times at Blackwater when silence rules, when the sound of human busyness is lost in the vastness of seemingly limitless marshes and a distant horizon. And then the sound of goose music breaks that silence, distant at first, then closer, as skeins of Canadas approach, swirl, and drop down, soon joined by other geese from every point of the compass, converging on Blackwater to create a cacophony that swells to the point where human conversation is impossible and you are lost in a blizzard of geese settling in for the night all around you. You are reminded that at such times the world seems young again, even immortal, free from the cares of human existence that so plague our species. Blackwater offers us the chance to reconnect with the natural world, the opportunity to renew our relationship with at least a few of the life forms that share our planet. If anywhere in Maryland is magical, the late autumn dusk at Blackwater is surely such a place.

Thousands of visitors to Blackwater tour the refuge by auto. Very few, however, paddle the tidal rivers by canoe or kayak. In recent years, the refuge has made canoeing and kayaking a more reasonable choice with the establishment of three designated paddling trails. Each has parking and easy access to the water. And despite their close proximity to each other, the trails differ enough to provide a unique perspective of Blackwater.

Before putting your boat in the water, visit the Blackwater National Wildlife Refuge Visitor Center on Key Wallace Drive. There are restrooms and water available here, but more importantly you can find out what time high tide is achieved, what the wind and weather predictions are, and whether hunting is going on along your planned route. The volunteer staff is knowledgeable and helpful, the displays are enlightening, the native plant gardens are well tended, and there is a fine gift shop.

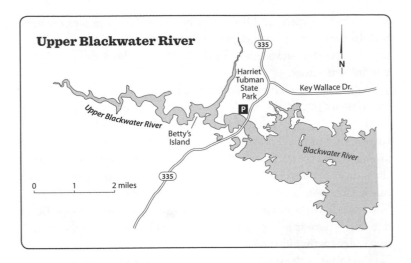

And while you are here to paddle, be sure to tour Wildlife Drive either before or after your trip. Even folks not much interested in birds will enjoy the two short walks available, the long views over the marsh, and the strong likelihood of seeing our national symbol, the bald eagle. Late afternoon is best; in autumn and winter, stay until dusk to see the immense flocks of geese returning to the refuge for the night.

Trip Description

Section 1: Route 335 to footbridge and return (green water trail)
Begin this paddling trip from the "trailhead" along Route 335 about a mile southwest from the intersection with Key Wallace Drive (about two miles from the Visitor Center). There is parking for more than a dozen cars but no other facilities. The upper Blackwater River is designated as the "green trail" by the refuge, although there are no signposts, buoys, or other markers along the way to guide you. Launch from the rocky beach, which is set up to preclude access by trailered boats with motors.

This initial portion of the upper Blackwater is a bay generally oval in shape and about a half mile across. Paddle toward the far end, opposite the Route 335 causeway. If the day is windy, you may want to stay near the shoreline, working your way around the edge of the bay. Note that when paddling in wind, a headwind makes for hard paddling but steering is not problematic, while wind from the stern or stern quarter makes steering difficult as the boat wallows in the windblown waves.

As you approach the far end of this bay, a relatively narrow opening appears to the left, marking the route for further progress upriver. From this point, look for and paddle toward Betty's Island. In the sea of marsh surrounding you on all sides, Betty's Island is an anomaly: an acre or two of high ground supporting tall loblolly pines that tower over everything else. It's a prominent and obvious landmark. Up close, it may be difficult to land and walk about on Betty's Island; tall, thick grasses and shrubs preclude easy access. Don't despair—there is a fine place to stretch your legs and enjoy lunch two miles further upriver.

Past Betty's Island, the upper Blackwater alternates between fairly wide bays and narrow passages. At low tide, avoid the points, where water is usually quite shallow, often marked by old tree stumps. The presence of these now long-dead trees in the water indicates that the sea level has risen at Blackwater within living memory, submerging what was once dry land beneath rising waters.

The waters of the upper Blackwater are fresh, without the taint of salt, permitting the surrounding marsh to support vegetation like narrow-leaved cattail and American threesquare. Cattails are familiar plants with thin, flat, unbranched leaves and a prominent flower spike. The narrow-leaved variety found here has a flower spike with a gap between its upper and lower sections. American threesquare is actually a sedge, with a distinctive triangular stem ("sedges have edges while rushes are round"). In colonial days, threesquare was used to cane chair seats. Although the marsh supports several other wetland plants, it is not as diverse as some other freshwater marshes, like those along the Patuxent River.

After about three miles of paddling, the river doglegs left and then right, narrowing considerably. Ahead, a wooden footbridge spans the river and marks the end of the official "green" paddling trail. This bridge is private property, so do not climb out onto it. The footbridge is constructed with one high spot, permitting small boats like kayaks and canoes to pass under. Energetic paddlers may wish to explore further upstream. In summer, a dense collection of water lilies clogs the water and limits progress, but there is at least one report that at a very high tide it is possible to cross over the height of land, portage across Taylors Island Road, and paddle into the waters of Chesapeake Bay!

After reaching the end of the refuge's official trail at the footbridge, return by the same route. Just before the first turn, there is solid land on the right that may provide an opportunity to get out of your boat and stretch. As of this writing, this area is not posted. A very pretty forest of mature pines and hardwoods form a high canopy, and Delmarva fox squirrels and pileated woodpeckers can sometimes be seen here. In any event, any beach up to the mean high tide point is public by Maryland law, and the low-tide beach here contains enough sand for a person to stand without sinking knee deep into marsh mud.

On the return trip, after the first mile of paddling, the high trees of Betty's Island provide a reference point for navigation. Once past Betty's, your car is just barely visible on the Route 335 causeway.

Section 2: Shorters Wharf upstream to near head of navigation and return (orange water trail) (Coles Creek)

Begin this trip from Shorters Wharf, located where Maple Dam Road crosses the Blackwater River on the downstream (southern) side of the refuge. There is parking here for perhaps a dozen cars, but there are no other facilities. Getting to this point by car is half the fun; the road is through the marsh on a causeway and has views in every direction of marsh grass, water, and a few distant trees. Maple Dam Road is just a few inches above the mean high tide mark; indeed, the road may be flooded when there is a northwest wind and a storm tide. The horizon is flat at every point of the compass. With good reason, this area is known as Maryland's Everglades, because the views are so similar.

Both the purple water trail and the orange water trail begin from Shorters Wharf. However, there are no signs here, and there is only one (at present, 2016) along the route. Launch from the boat ramp, ideally about two hours before high tide. That allows the tide to enhance your paddling to the orange water trail's end, at which time the tide turns and runs the other way for your reverse trip. If that ideal situation does not occur, don't despair. The tidal flux is weak enough to paddle against; only in combination with a strong breeze (above about 8 mph) will paddling be problematical. On the other hand, a breeze is useful. Blackwater is one of the buggiest places in Maryland, and a breeze might keep some of the winged hordes at bay. Even so, bring insect repellent and consider a spring or fall (after first frost) trip.

Leaving the boat ramp and heading upstream, away from the bridge, the river is about fifty yards wide. It is lined with a wall of big cordgrass, a native grass that can grow to heights of twelve feet. Big cordgrass roots bind the marsh together, and at low tide that beneficial ability is easily viewed. Geese eat the stout rhizome, and muskrats use the stems to construct their lodges. King rails and Virginia rails may occasionally be seen at low tide, emerging from the deep vegetation to feed atop the exposed mudflats.

A few feet behind the scrim of big cordgrass are extensive wetland meadows made up almost exclusively of salt marsh cordgrass. Only a foot or two in height, salt marsh cordgrass is the dominant plant in salt and brackish water tidal marshes; it covers thousands of acres of the Chesapeake Bay wetlands. Interestingly, it is able to grow in higher salinity water better than big cordgrass. So why doesn't salt marsh cordgrass replace big cordgrass at the water's edge? The roots of big cordgrass are inundated twice every day, but salt marsh cordgrass here at Blackwater sees water only occasionally, at very high tides. As that water recedes and the marsh dries, the salt left behind is actually at a higher concentration than the salt in the river water.

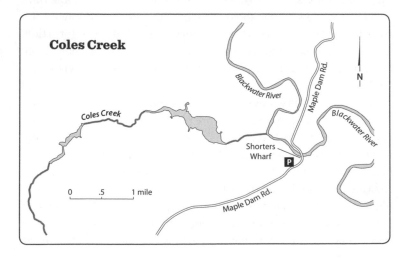

After a bit less than a mile of paddling, bear left at the first branch, into Coles Creek. Coming in from the right is the actual Blackwater River, but neither the orange nor the purple water trail follows its course upriver. The water trail soon opens up into a wide bay, where a windy day can make paddling difficult; stay near the lee edge of the marsh, where the vegetation can give some small degree of shelter.

A second branch point is reached after another mile of paddling. Again, stay left for the orange water trail; the purple water trail goes right. There may be a directional sign at this location, but such signs rarely last long in this windy location, anchored only in mud. Continue paddling up Coles Creek, which eventually narrows to the same fifty-yard width as at the put-in. Shortly after this, your one opportunity to land, get out, and stretch your legs may be found on the right, where Blackwater Road reaches the water's edge. Judging by a few pilings in the river, this was once the site of a footbridge, now long gone. Note that Blackwater Road is merely a packed gravel affair a few inches higher than the surrounding marsh; it is also gated, so only emergency vehicles ever get back here.

Continue paddling upriver. Two changes soon occur. First, the river becomes shallow; your paddle stroke often raises a swirl of mud. At mid-tide, it can feel as if you are paddling in molasses when the water is only a foot or less in depth. At low tide, you may have to search for the channel, as the rest of the river is too shallow to paddle. Second, the vegetation begins to change, since this more upstream reach is fresher still. Narrow leaved cattails begin to replace the cordgrasses, and in a few areas *Phragmites*, the common reed, has colonized the marsh. Islands of loblolly pines dot the landscape. The ones closer to the water are often dead, their woody skeletons outlined against the sky. Blackwater has thousands of such standing snags, killed by rising water levels (due to global warming) and land subsidence.

Coles Creek eventually takes a dogleg, left and then right, and soon thereafter reaches the end of the official paddling trail at Loblolly Landing, marked by a large and conspicuous tree stand erected on a ridge of dry land. This is private property, so do not disembark. Although it is possible to continue paddling upriver, Coles Creek soon dissolves into a place that is neither land nor water, marking the head of small boat navigation. Return to Shorters Wharf by the same route.

Section 3: Shorters Wharf to Route 335 (purple water trail)

Although this is an official water trail of Blackwater National Wildlife Refuge, I do not recommend it. Most of the route is in open water several miles wide, and conditions are usually quite windy. Furthermore, this open area is shallow; at low tide, much of it is mud flats. At higher tides, the route is difficult to discern because the mud flats are covered with only a few inches of water. On a sinking tide, you could find yourself aground on a mud flat with no choice but to wait four or five hours for the next rising tide. Finally, the purple water trail is closed October 1 through March 31, to avoid disturbing the waterfowl that rest here. From May to closure at the end of September, bugs and heat can be a problem. If you decide that you simply must paddle the purple trail, a calm day in April might be the best choice. Since it is nine miles one way, having two cars and doing a vehicle shuttle is preferable to an eighteen-mile, out-and-back marathon paddling trip.

Directions

From Baltimore or Washington, DC, cross the Chesapeake Bay Bridge on Route 50 and continue to Cambridge, Maryland. As you leave Cambridge, turn right on Woods Road. Go 0.9 miles, then turn right on Route 16. Proceed 16 miles to the little crossroads of Church Creek. Turn left on Route 335. Go 3.9 miles to Key Wallace Drive. Turn left; the Visitor Center is 1.0 miles ahead on the right.

To reach the put-in for the green water trail, leave the Visitor Center, turning left on Key Wallace Drive. Go 1.0 miles and turn left on Route 335. Proceed about a mile to the well-marked put-in parking lot on the right.

To reach the put-in for the orange and purple water trails, leave the Visitor Center, turning right on Key Wallace Drive. Go 2.6 miles, then turn right on Maple Dam Road. Proceed 5.3 miles to Shorters Wharf, on the right.

Other Outdoor Recreational Opportunities Nearby

Touring the refuge's Wildlife Drive by car or bicycle is quite popular and enjoyable. For paddlers, Transquaking Creek is located less than a 15-minute drive away (see a full description elsewhere in this book). Harriet Tubman State Park has some interesting displays and information and is located about a mile from the Blackwater NWR Visitor Center.

CLIMATE CHANGE AND THE
BLACKWATER MARSHES

I paddle my canoe past the cordgrass marshes, the autumn sun reaching toward the horizon, setting the tawny grasses aglow with a golden light. Here on the Blackwater River in Dorchester County, as remote a place as exists in Maryland, the hand of humans seems an inconsequential thing. This marsh appears to be the same lonely place it has been since I started visiting here almost forty years ago, nothing but marsh grass and water and a few distant pine islands decorating the far horizon. It might seem that if change comes here at all, it will come slowly, creeping along in incremental stages too minor for a human to detect in one lifetime.

And yet, it is not so. Change is an inevitable part of life, and perhaps nowhere in Maryland is that change more significant than in these lovely marshes. That change is subtle, however, not obvious like when a grove of trees is removed for yet another housing development. But subtle is nonetheless real.

The clues become obvious with time and experience. The edge of the wetland, where marsh reaches forest, is studded with the barren trunks of long-dead loblolly pines. In a place that is neither soil nor water, life is difficult, and many of these trees have given up the ghost. Places that were once living marsh, rich with life, are now water at high tide and mud at low. Lake Blackwater, they now call it. What was more than 5,000 acres of grasses, sedges, and rushes, is now gone, all gone.

Water levels are rising in the Blackwater River watershed—more than a foot in the last century. By 2100, some models indicate a further rise of as much as three feet. For these marshes, and for Dorchester County, it will be a disaster; maps show the entire southwestern part of this low-lying county will be converted entirely to water. The cause: primarily global warming. A rise in global temperatures will melt more of the polar ice caps, raising sea levels significantly. It's happened before on planet Earth—we have many kinds of evidence to show that it has—but never at so fast a pace. Human activity, especially the burning of fossil fuels, is warming the planet's atmosphere at an unprecedented rate, and that global warming has effects everywhere around the globe—even here at Blackwater, as untrammeled a place as exists in the Free State.

Late in 2016, a project began at Blackwater that may be able to, in part, offset those marshland losses. It's an experiment, the results of which are unknown and even unpredictable, but the scientists who designed it hope that useful lessons can be learned even if the experiment is unsuccessful. A barge anchored in the river near Shorters Wharf is dredging sand, mud, and organic matter from the river bottom and spewing it out over the adjacent dying marsh. The goal is to increase the level of soil in the wetlands by one foot over the winter. In late spring, the dormant marsh grasses should still be able to grow up through the new sludge. Scientists will monitor the return of vegetation, the degree to which the new soil is eroded by tides, and the hoped-for return of marsh birds like the saltmarsh sparrow and black rail. Can this technique be used to mitigate some of these marshland losses to global warming? Or is what has happened in the past an inevitable predictor of what will happen in the future? Only time will tell.

Transsquaking River

River Section: From Bestpitch Boat Ramp downstream and return (loop)
County: Dorchester
Distance: About 5 miles
Difficulty: Easy except when windy. Tidal flatwater
Hazards: Winds, strong tides, biting insects
Tide Information: https://tidesandcurrents.noaa.gov/tide_predictions.html;
    select Maryland and scroll to the McCready's Creek station
Highlights: An isolated and lightly visited brackish marsh exhibiting
    interesting wetland vegetation and birds
Nearby Canoe/Kayak Rental: None
More Information: Maryland Department of Natural Resources,
    Heritage and Wildlife Service, (410) 260-8540
Street Address: 3706 Bestpitch Ferry Road, Cambridge, Maryland 21613
GPS Coordinates: 38.415676, 75.994025 (Bestpitch Boat Ramp)

W ay down in a remote corner of Dorchester County, far from the maddening crowd of even small towns, lies an extensive marshland, a place that is neither land nor water, where the view across wetland meadows of *Spartina* and *Juncus* and *Scirpus* are so far-reaching that it resembles the wetlands of south Florida. These brackish tidal marshes cover tens of thousands of acres and drain into Fishing Bay, part of Tangier Sound and Chesapeake Bay proper. A trip by canoe or kayak into the waterways that wind through these marshes and drain into Fishing Bay allows the paddler to experience one of the least-visited places in Maryland, where humans are only rare sightseers, and where, as one wag said, "if it's not the end of the world, at least you can see it from here."

Paddling these marshes can be a difficult endeavor. The wider rivers around Fishing Bay are more suitable to power boats, owing

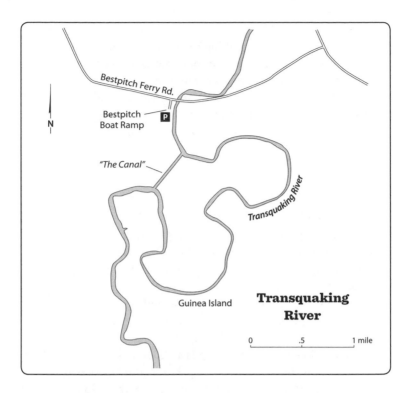

Bestpitch Ferry Rd.

Bestpitch
Boat Ramp

N

"The Canal"

Transquaking River

Guinea Island   **Transquaking
River**

0   .5   1 mile

to the long distances between land access points and an often vigorous tidal flux. The smaller creeks, in addition, are labyrinthine; route finding can be challenging, and getting lost is a real possibility. And then there are the bugs. From May through first frost, lower Dorchester County seems to harbor more, and more kinds of, biting, annoying, frustrating, just plain drive-you-crazy insects than anywhere short of the Arctic tundra.

So why would anyone come to paddle here? To a special kind of person, one who values untrammeled wildness, lonely corners where few humans care to go, unusual plants and animals, and scenery that is quietly spectacular, the marshes of lower Dorchester rival the mountains of Garrett County and the seashore at Assateague. The key is to be thoroughly prepared to paddle here: use the tides to your advantage, visit in spring or fall when insect life is at least tolerable, have the skills to navigate your chosen route, and above all possess the paddling ability and common sense to carry out a safe and enjoyable trip.

Of the many possible locations to canoe or kayak in the Fishing Bay watershed, the Transquaking River offers some positive attributes. First, the route described is long enough to get a feel for these marshes, but short enough to paddle in three or four hours. Unusual for this area, there is a place to get out to stretch and snack about halfway through the trip. Best of all, this is a circuit trip rather than an out-and-back, so that new vistas appear for most of your time in the boat.

Trip Description

Begin your paddling trip from the Bestpitch Boat Ramp, managed by Maryland's Department of Natural Resources. There is a large paved lot with plenty of parking, but no other facilities. Note that after storms and at very high tides the paved road into Bestpitch may be covered with water; do not try to drive through standing water. (Furthermore, at such times you really should not be on the water in a small, human-powered boat.) Put your canoe or kayak in the water at the same concrete ramp used by power boats.

The ideal time to begin this trip is an hour or so before low tide. That will permit you to ride the last of the receding tide downstream (toward Fishing Bay). When the tide turns, it will then aid you in your return to Bestpitch. Conversely, should the tide be against you for a majority of your trip, expect to have to paddle hard to make progress. Wind can also be a factor during the first mile of this trip, where the river is wider, straighter, and more exposed. Finally, note that, unlike some other water trails, the Transquaking Loop is unmarked.

From your launch site, paddle downstream, away from the wooden bridge that carries Bestpitch Ferry Road over the river. Within a half mile, bear right at a fork, entering what is known locally as "the Canal." This section is straight, dredged years ago to shorten the route between the Bestpitch boat ramp and Fishing Bay. Dredging this half-mile section of marsh eliminated more than three miles of the sinuous route taken by the Transquaking River. The Canal is where wind and tide, if against you, will be the most bothersome.

At the next fork, after about a mile of paddling, bear left into what was the original riverbed of the Transquaking, before the Canal made it into an oxbow. The wetland to your left is called Thoroughfare Marsh, and it is a beautiful example of the brackish marshes so common in the Fishing Bay watershed. The water here is neither fresh nor salty, but a mixture that is about halfway on the salinity scale. Furthermore, that salinity will vary depending on how much fresh water (from rainfall in the headwaters of the watershed) dilutes the brackish water around Thoroughfare Marsh. Thus, wetland plants must be adapted to range of salinities.

Another mile of paddling brings you to some high ground, where marsh gives way to loblolly pines. Known as Guinea Island, this chunk of ground provides your one chance to get out of your boat, walk around, enjoy a snack, and get a view of the surrounding marshes from the only patch of dry land for quite some distance. Use care, however; ticks and poison ivy are common. Avoid high grass and thick underbrush, and don't touch any hairy vine. Native Americans once used this island, judging by the presence of oyster middens that have been found here.

Continue paddling in a generally northerly direction, although the many loops of the Transquaking traverse every point of the compass. Feel free to explore some of the many guts, or small tidal creeks, that flow into the main river. It is in these narrow, twisty passages where you'll get to experience the marsh in a visceral way, and where you might find red-winged blackbirds, ducks, and rails. Indeed, the marshes around Fishing Bay are the last refuge of the federally endangered black rail, a sparrow-sized marsh bird so rare it was not even photographed on the nest until 1987.

After a bit over four miles total of paddling, you'll arrive back at the first fork, at the origin of the Canal. Turn right and paddle back to the boat launch at Bestpitch.

Directions

From the Bay Bridge, take Route 50 through Cambridge. Turn right at Bucktown Road (also marked as the airport exit). Follow Bucktown Road south for about six miles. Turn left onto Bestpitch Ferry Road and travel about four miles. Just before crossing the bridge over the Transquaking River, turn right onto the Fishing Bay Wildlife Management Area entrance road, and follow it to the boat launch parking lot at the end.

Other Outdoor Recreational Opportunities Nearby

Blackwater National Wildlife Refuge is about a 15-minute drive from Bestpitch and offers superb bird and wildlife watching. Wildlife Drive may also be cycled, providing a different way to see the refuge. There are two good paddle trails at Blackwater as well, described elsewhere in this book.

OYSTERS

What comes to mind at the mention of the words "Chesapeake Bay"? Crabs? Sailing? The Orioles? Fishing? The Naval Academy? Watermen? For decades, the Chesapeake was also synonymous with oysters, those tasty bivalves that were a staple of colonial diets and a gourmet's delight through the 1970s. But soon thereafter, decades of overharvesting, disease, and high nutrient levels caught up to the species, and by 2005 the oyster industry in Maryland was on life support.

At the time Captain John Smith sailed into Chesapeake Bay, oysters were an incredibly abundant natural resource. Oyster bars were hazards to navigation and covered immense portions of the Bay's bottom. Prehistoric middens have yielded shells up to 10 inches long, and early travelers reported that they had to cut oyster meats in half to eat them. Oysters are filter feeders, and by one estimate the oyster population of Chesapeake Bay at that time could filter (and thus purify) all the water in the Bay in less than a week. In contrast, the oysters remaining at the start of the twenty-first century would require almost a year to perform the same task.

Oysters are in decline in Chesapeake Bay for three reasons: overharvesting, pollution, and disease. For almost a century, watermen strip-mined the Bay's shallows for oysters. Harvests reached a peak in 1884 at almost 15 million bushels and slowly declined thereafter to a steady-state harvest of about 2 million bushels annually between 1935 and 1980. Thereafter, harvests declined again, falling to about 27,000 bushels in 2004. The same kinds of pollution problems that plague other organisms in Chesapeake Bay have an even greater impact on oysters. Nutrient enrichment that results in oxygen-depleted water spells trouble for immobile oysters, as do increased sediment loads, which cover suitable habitat and smother living oysters. Finally, two oyster parasites, MSX, a protozoan, and Dermo, a fungus, have killed immense number of oysters. By 2005, watermen, scientists, conservationists, and managers all thought the oyster industry was dying, and that oysters would no longer play a role in the ecology of the Bay.

But they were wrong. The oyster has made an astonishing comeback in the decade since its nadir. In 2014, almost a million bushels were harvested baywide. The number of watermen who harvest oysters has doubled. The harvest looks guardedly sustainable. What has caused this dramatic turnaround?

After decades of infection with Dermo and MSX, the surviving oysters have evolved some level of immunity, and the population as a whole is less susceptible to these diseases. A series of years without floods have kept nutrient levels free from spikes, and sediment input relatively low. But the most important change has been to establish oyster sanctuaries, where, by Maryland law, watermen may not harvest the oyster rocks. By 2016, almost 9,000 acres, or 24 percent of the Bay's suitable oyster habitat, had been set aside.

These oyster sanctuaries are based on the idea that oysters are more than just food for human consumption and a way for watermen to make a living off the Bay. Scientists recognize that oysters are a keystone species in the ecology of Chesapeake Bay. Oyster bars are a distinct habitat, harboring a rich assemblage of other species dependent on the bar for food and shelter. More oysters, unmolested year-round, remove more algae and prevent oxygen depletion. Even the physical size of oyster bars are beneficial, breaking up wave energy during storms that otherwise might cause erosion. The positive attributes of oyster sanctuaries are many, and should continue to contribute to the recovery of oysters baywide.

Tuckahoe Creek

River Section: Section 1: Crouse Mill Lake upstream to head of navigation
and return
Section 2: Crouse Mill Dam downstream to Hillsboro
Counties: Queen Anne, Caroline
Distance: Section 1: About 5 miles
Section 2: 5.2 miles
Difficulty: Section 1: Easy. Flat, with some slowly flowing water
Section 2: Easy to moderate. Mostly flowing water, with some tidal
flatwater near the end
Hazards: Section 1: None
Section 2: Trees down in river, poison ivy
Highlights: Section 1: A nontidal freshwater marsh rich in wildlife, blending
into a shady mature riparian forest
Section 2: A narrow and intimate creek running through a beautiful
riparian forest
Nearby Canoe/Kayak Rental: Tuckahoe State Park, (410) 820-1668
More Information: Tuckahoe State Park, dnr.maryland.gov/publiclands
/Pages/eastern/Tuckahoe.aspx, (410) 820-1668
Street Address: Near 13070 Crouse Mill Road, Queen Anne, Maryland 21657
GPS Coordinates: 38.967066, 75.942727 (Crouse Mill Road at the dam)

A mong the earliest signs of a Chesapeake springtime is the
migration of anadromous fish from the ocean to their breeding grounds in narrow headwater streams. All around the Chesapeake Bay drainage, fish crowd the shallows, congregating at rapids,
dams, and other obstructions. Seining, dipnetting, and fishing for
shad, white perch, yellow perch, rockfish, and river herring at these
places is a Chesapeake tradition, still another way for Marylanders
to connect with the cycles of the natural world. The numbers of all

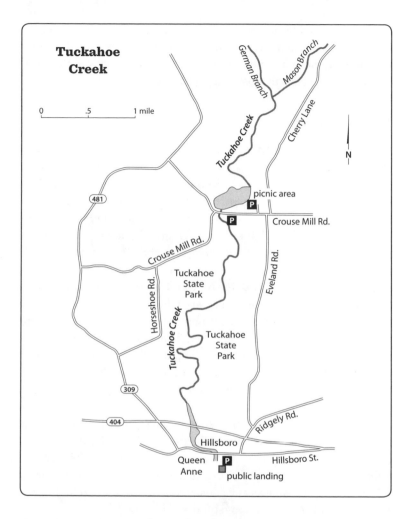

these fish species have declined precipitously in the last thirty years, but even today a few creeks and rivers play host to ever-dwindling stocks. Tuckahoe Creek, forming the border between Queen Anne and Caroline Counties, is one of the best of these places. Blessed by good water quality and protected by wooded buffers over much of its nontidal length, the Tuckahoe is a wild and beautiful river.

Paddling the Tuckahoe is a fine way to spend the day in almost any season. Set amid a vast expanse of the mid-Shore's mostly agricultural landscape, it is a haven for wildlife. Paddlers can choose to navigate a narrow, intimate stream, flowing quickly through forested bottomlands to tidewater, or explore a drowned swamp forest where sunlight has created a rich and diverse open marsh. And despite its relatively close proximity to the metropolitan areas to the west, Tuckahoe Creek is still mostly undiscovered.

Trip Description

Section 1: Crouse Mill Lake Upriver

This segment of Tuckahoe Creek is the section of choice if you do not want to run a vehicle shuttle or in the event that section 2 is too low owing to extended drought. It is possible to paddle about 2.5 miles upriver, almost to where German Branch and Mason Branch unite to form the Tuckahoe. This situation changes episodically, however, when storms bring down large trees that span the creek. The Park Service usually clears out these "strainers" promptly.

Put your canoe or kayak in the water at Tuckahoe State Park's lakeside picnic area, where there are wheelchair-accessible bathrooms. Alternatively, there is a launch ramp with no facilities on the opposite side of the 60-acre lake. Paddle across the pond and to the right, where a wide expanse of marshland forms the upper reaches of the lake. Explore gaps in the vegetation until you find a lead that opens upriver. Tuckahoe's inlet is mazelike, but many channels eventually coalesce into the main creek.

In late fall and winter, the lake is home to large flocks of ducks and geese. Dabbling ducks like mallards, pintails, and widgeons feed on vegetation in the shallow waters; geese loaf here in safety before flying out into the nearby agricultural fields to feed. Even in summer, a few families of mallards and geese hang out in the little millpond, attracted by the open water and plentiful food.

Within a few bends of the stream is a beaver lodge, constructed mostly of sticks. It is quite large, about eight feet in diameter and almost four feet in height above the waterline. Beaver are now common in most streams in Maryland after being reintroduced by the Department of Natural Resources. In areas such as this one, where there is no significant flow to the river but abundant food, beaver can exist happily without building dams.

This section of the wetland once had a number of trees, but construction of the dam and lake inundated the roots and killed them. Thus, there are many dead snags, which form perches for kingfishers, herons, red-winged blackbirds, kingbirds, and hawks. Woodpeckers have drilled holes in some of them for nest cavities, which are also utilized by starlings.

Other snags look almost alive, as tangles of poison ivy vines have climbed them to great heights. At water level, hammocks of vegetation have organized around some of the old stumps; swamp rose, with pink flowers, and water hemlock, with clusters of white umbrella-shaped flowers, predominate here. Along the edges of the creek, water dock and lizard's tail form the herbaceous layer. Spatterdock, pickerelweed, and cattail, the predominant vegetation of most freshwater marshes on the Eastern Shore, are present but are of lesser importance, probably because this marsh is nontidal.

After several hundred yards of paddling, more trees begin to encroach on the marsh, and the creek becomes partially shaded. Red maples are the dominant tree, although there are plenty of specimens of green ash and black gum. Silky dogwood, a water-loving shrub with leaves that look like the more familiar dogwood of lawns and forest, lines the banks. Although the flowers are small and clustered rather than singular, each has the same four petals. Bluish berries form later in the season. Wood ducks and prothonotary warblers like these forested swamps.

The creek soon narrows to about 20 feet in width and becomes shallower. In a few places, it may become so shallow that your boat scrapes the bottom, but persist onward since the stream soon deepens. Aquatic grasses of several types line the riverbed, indicating good water quality. Bottom sediments are gravel and coarse sand rather than mud; this well-oxygenated substrate is favored as spawning beds and nest sites by anadromous fish.

After almost two miles of upriver travel, several concrete steps may be seen on the right. These lead to the campfire area of the state park's youth group campground. Another half mile or so of paddling inevitably brings you to a tree spanning the entire river and blocking further passage. Although you can portage, strainers appear ever more frequently upriver, making this a good place to turn around.

Section 2: Crouse Mill Dam to Hillsboro

This 5.2-mile section of the Tuckahoe begins at the foot of Crouse Mill Dam, just downstream from section 1. It is remarkably different in character, flowing tight and twisty through a deep swamp forest and then emerging into the sunlight at tidewater. The Tuckahoe is usually runnable all year long, although the water is low in dry summers and it may then be necessary to carry your boat over a few shallow gravel beds and submerged logs. The rangers and volunteers of Tuckahoe State Park periodically cut out trees that fall across the creek; judging by all the work they've done in the past, this little stream would be an impassable tangle if not for their efforts.

Unload your canoe or kayak where the creek passes under Crouse Mill Road. There is roadside parking here but no other facilities, although the picnic area restrooms are only a hundred yards away. This is an extraordinarily popular place for fishing in late March through mid-April, when anadromous fish migrating to their upstream spawning grounds cluster at the base of the dam's fish ladder. Shad, perch, and river herring all use the upper Tuckahoe; to see their silvery forms dashing upriver over gravel beds is one of the classic harbingers of a Chesapeake spring.

The Tuckahoe flows off into the forest at a slow but steady pace; only at high water could the current cause problems. Just a few yards wide, the creek twists around sharp turns and under overhanging tree limbs and fallen trunks. Each is festooned with a dense covering of poison ivy, without a doubt the most dangerous feature of this trip. Poison ivy is easily identified by its leaves in groups of three; in winter, avoid touching any hairy vine. Vireos, wood thrushes, cardinals, and other woodland songbirds abound in the adjacent forested bottomlands. Hawks and owls nest in these riparian greenways, flying out to feed in nearby abandoned fields. In the summer, butterflies brighten the gloom as they flit through the understory, and dragonflies patrol the river. Mosquitoes, deerflies, and horseflies are common, especially in late spring and early summer, so bring along insect repellent.

After about two miles of narrow river, the stream runs up against a high, steep cliff bank, scoured smooth and free of vegetation, on the right-hand side of the river. This marks the entrance to a wider, deeper pool section of the river. Turtles, including huge old snappers, abound in this area. Within a few hundred yards, the river reverts to its narrower, more winding character, persisting like this for about another mile and a half.

A unique aspect of the Tuckahoe is its river bottom. Large portions of it are covered with small black stones, rounded and water worn, larger than gravel but not big enough to be called rocks. Such stones are unusual on the Coastal Plain, where unconsolidated sands and gravels are the rule. High water probably flushes away the gravel and sand but is not strong enough to move the rocks, leaving portions of the river bottom with a cobbled effect. Freshwater clams and mussels also abound among the Tuckahoe's cobbles. Small shells, less than an inch in diameter, accumulate in the eddys, but large empty shells up to three inches long litter the river bottom in other places. The shells, which remain far beyond the animals' lifespan, are testimony to a flourishing benthic community in the Tuckahoe's riverbed.

The Tuckahoe eventually reaches tidewater, where the river noticeably widens, from 20 feet to 20 yards. However, this size is still relatively intimate for a tidal stream, and so the creek remains a pleasant paddle. With sunlight hitting the river, the vegetation changes; shrubs and small trees like sweetbay magnolia, buttonbush, and alder line the banks; a few pocket marshes feature wild rice and wild iris. In the last quarter mile, the Tuckahoe passes under two abandoned railroad bridges and two road bridges. Take out at the public landing at Hillsboro.

Directions

From Baltimore or Washington, DC, cross the Bay Bridge and continue on Route 50 south. Turn left onto Route 404 and continue east for 6.8 miles. Turn left on Ridgely Road, at a stoplight. Go 100 yards and turn left on Eveland Road. Go to the end, and turn left on Crouse Mill Road. Follow this road to the picnic area, the dam, and its lake. To reach Hillsboro, return to Ridgely Road but continue across Route 404. The road ends within 150 yards, in Hillsboro. Turn right; the landing is on the left just before crossing the bridge.

Other Outdoor Recreational Opportunities Nearby

There are over ten miles of hiking trails in Tuckahoe State Park. Adkins Arboretum also has several miles of walking trails, is excellent for birding and wildflowers, and is located only a five-minute drive from the Tuckahoe millpond.

DELMARVA FOX SQUIRRELS

The sound of rustling leaves disturbs my reverie as I walk through this lovely forest in Talbot County. It's just a squirrel, rooting though the autumn-dry leaves, looking for beechnuts. But something about this squirrel gives me pause, and I take a second look; it's paler than the gray squirrels I see around my house every day; it has beautiful silver fur with a white underbelly. And it's large, significantly larger than gray squirrels. I realize that, given this mid-Shore location, I'm looking at a Delmarva fox squirrel.

A subspecies of the common fox squirrel, Delmarvas are robust, the largest squirrel in North America. They have prominent ears, very bushy tails, and a light gray pelage. When disturbed, Delmarvas tend to run across the forest floor rather than head up the nearest tree. Accordingly, they require mature forests with large trees and a minimal shrub/sapling layer. They do not adapt well to modern society, having the unfortunate propensity of dashing across a road and under the tires of oncoming vehicles. Some call them "suicide squirrels," and several have been killed even along the dirt roads of nature centers here by cars doing less than the 15 mph speed limit.

By the mid-twentieth century, Delmarva fox squirrels were in serious trouble, occupying just 10 percent of their historic range. In large measure, this decline was due to the loss of habitat; mature forests, with trees more than a century old, had mostly been cut down for timber or farmland. Once found throughout the Eastern Shore, by the mid-sixties these squirrels could only be located in four counties in the mid-Shore region. Accordingly, the US Fish and Wildlife Service placed the Delmarva fox squirrel on the original endangered species list in 1967.

Given the attention that accompanied listing, scientists devised plans to recover the species. Staff at the Maryland Department of Natural Resources began a translocation program in the 1980s, trapping excess Delmarvas from areas with good population sizes and relocating them to areas of suitable habitat. One early success was at Chincoteague National Wildlife Refuge in Virginia, just a few miles south of the Maryland border. The program was aided by the willingness of the squirrels to use artificial nest boxes; within a decade, more than 500 Delmarva fox squirrels populated a loblolly pine forest at the refuge. Most of the transplants, however, went to private property owners willing to help with the recovery program, because most of the suitable habitat was in private rather than public hands. Given the concern expressed about the restrictions placed on development of private land by the Endangered Species Act, the participation of private landowners was unexpected but very welcome, testimony to the affection these beautiful creatures inspire. By 2014, Delmarvas occupied 28 percent of suitable habitat on the Shore and were no longer considered in danger of extirpation. Accordingly, the Delmarva fox squirrel was removed from the endangered species list in December 2015.

Nanjemoy Creek

River Section: Section 1: Friendship Landing to head of navigation on
Church Creek
Section 2: Friendship Landing to head of navigation on Hill Top Fork
Section 3: Friendship Landing to head of navigation on Nanjemoy Creek
County: Charles
Distance: Section 1: 3 miles round trip
Section 2: 5 miles round trip
Section 3: 11 miles round trip
Difficulty: Easy except when windy. Tidal flatwater
Hazards: Windy weather possible
Tide Information: https://tidesandcurrents.noaa.gov/tide_predictions.html;
select Maryland and scroll to the Riverside station
Highlights: An extensive and biodiverse freshwater marsh with forested
borders in a rural corner of Maryland
Nearby Canoe/Kayak Rental: None
More Information: None
Street Address: 4715 Friendship Landing Road, Nanjemoy, Maryland 20662
GPS Coordinates: 38.454172, 77.150528 (boat ramp launch site)

Paddling the tidal rivers and creeks of the Chesapeake Bay drainage can be a surprising delight. Most people look out over a vast expanse of marsh or into a tangle of fallen trees in a wooded swamp and think one thing: bugs. For the most part, they're wrong. Oh, there are plenty of insects out there, but relatively few are of the biting variety. Only in the salt marshes of the lower Eastern Shore are bugs a major problem, and then only on dead calm days near the vegetation. Freshwater marshes and swamps have much smaller populations of mosquitoes, and they are most bothersome in late spring, with their numbers declining significantly with the onset of hot, dry

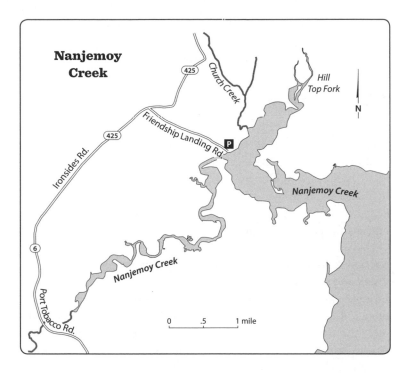

weather. Furthermore, such insects seem to avoid the cooler air over water, so the route that you, as a paddler, want to take will be the least buggy. In short, don't let an irrational fear of insects keep you from the joys of paddling the dense green jungles of our freshwater swamps and marshes.

Nanjemoy Creek, in Charles County, is just such a place. From the put-in at Friendship Landing Park, you might never suspect you'll soon be paddling in a marsh. At this point, the Nanjemoy is a wide estuary, the view leading to the distant Potomac River, melting into a haze where the separation between air and water is tenuous and uncertain. But launch your kayak or canoe, head either left or right, and you'll eventually reach a place where the route dissolves into a tangle of buttonbush, where smartweed reaches over the gunnels, and where spiders drop into your boat for a visit. You may be surprised to find that you are willing to hop out on a beaver-chewed log and haul your boat over it just so you can gain another dozen yards of progress. Knee deep sucking mud becomes a fact of life. These are the exquisite charms of swampin'.

The Nanjemoy estuary offers three choices for paddling trips, all from the same launch site: short, moderate, and long. Surely one will prove suitable for your experience and energy level.

Trip Description

Begin each of these trips from Friendship Landing Park, where there is parking for a dozen or more cars (depending on how many power boat trailers occupy the lot). A portable toilet sits about 100 yards back up the hill, hidden by a privacy fence, but there are no other facilities. Launching is easy; Charles County has provided a launch cradle for kayaks. Put your craft in the polyethylene cradle, hop in, and use the handrails to pull you and your boat into the water.

Section 1: Friendship Landing to head of navigation on Church Creek and return

From the launch site, turn left, following the shoreline. In the event of significant wind, this trip may be the best choice since it is the most sheltered of the three options, but even so, the first mile is quite open. The first break in the riverside bank is on the left and leads into the more sheltered portions of what is now called Church Creek. (The headwaters of this little stream originate from Durham Church, one of the original thirty parishes chartered by the State of Maryland in 1692.)

Church Creek winds through a broad marsh in lazy, S-shaped bends for about another half mile, getting progressively narrower. As a river or stream flows, its water tends to move faster at the outer edge of a curve, eroding the soil of the adjacent stream bank. On the inside of the curve, water moves more slowly, and thus deposits its sediment load. The result is that, over time, a stream becomes increasingly sinuous. On such a creek, you may find yourself paddling through at least 180 degrees of the compass at each bend.

The marsh at Church Creek is dominated by big cordgrass, *Spartina cynosuroides*. This perennial grass grows up to a dozen feet in height and is easily distinguished by its comb-shaped seed heads. Even though Church Creek (and Nanjemoy Creek) are a fair distance from the brackish waters of Chesapeake Bay, the presence of big cordgrass indicates a slight amount of salinity in the water.

Eventually, the creek narrows to just a few feet in width, and at this point the marsh vegetation becomes more diverse. Crimson-eyed rose mallow is common, and at midsummer its large white flowers make the marsh resemble a cotton field. Buttonbush is another easily identified marsh plant; its spherical flowers and fruits, although only a modest inch in diameter, attract a variety of native pollinators. By autumn, tickseed sunflowers and swamp asters lend a wash of color to the marsh.

Push your way into the marsh as far as you are able. The rewards are an intimate look at a location few people get to experience, a place with life in abundance. Insects and spiders (few are of the biting variety) abound, water snakes, turtles, and frogs are common if rarely seen up close, and there is usually a well-hidden beaver lodge. Overhead, bald eagles, kingfishers, and red-shouldered hawks are often heard year-round, while ospreys and laughing gulls are summer residents. When you can't go any farther, back out (if there's room to turn around, you haven't gone far enough into the marsh!), and return to Friendship Landing by the same route, for a round-trip distance of almost 3 miles. The same cradle used to launch can also be used for landing.

Section 2: Friendship Landing to head of navigation on Hill Top Fork and return

This route is a bit longer than the Church Creek circuit but is not appreciably different in character. It too begins on the wide portion of Nanjemoy Creek, becomes increasingly narrow, and ends in a maze-like marsh. Thirty years ago, this trip was more popular because one of the eastern United States's largest great blue heron rookeries then occupied the upper reaches of Hill Top Fork. For reasons not fully understood, the herons abandoned this rookery site and likely moved to a new location across the Potomac River in Virginia.

From Friendship Landing, paddle across the wide Nanjemoy estuary toward a long dock on the far shore. This crossing can be difficult on a windy day, so use discretion. Then turn left, following the shoreline in a northerly direction. Mature trees atop sloping uplands well above mean high tide ensure some degree of shelter from the wind. Hill Top Fork soon becomes narrower and meanders, each turn revealing new sights; a few acres of marsh host wild rice, while others have been invaded by the common reed, *Phragmites*. Eventually, further progress will require paddling through dense thickets of rushes, cattails, small shrubs, and wetland wildflowers, thus constituting the most enjoyable and interesting part of the trip. When you run out of water, return to Friendship Landing by the same route.

Section 3: Friendship Landing to head of navigation on Nanjemoy Creek and return

The final route of this trio of paddling trips is the longest and eventually attains the wooded headwaters of Nanjemoy Creek proper. Some reaches of Nanjemoy are fairly narrow, providing shelter from wind, but other parts are more exposed. Still, only a few segments might prove problematical on windy days.

Again, begin your paddle from Friendship Landing, but this time turn right. Within 100 yards, you'll leave the wide open spaces of the estuary to enjoy the narrower confines of the creek proper. On many days, yours will not be the only boat on Nanjemoy Creek; it is a popular place for largemouth bass fishing. Like much of the Potomac River below Washington, DC, Nanjemoy Creek has seen improving water quality (from upgrades to the Blue Plains sewage treatment plant) that has permitted the growth of underwater grasses. These grasses, like coontail, hornwort, and hydrilla, shelter a diverse assemblage of small fish that in turn support predator fish like largemouths. The Nanjemoy Creek watershed is still very rural, with more than 80 percent of the land in forest, ensuring clean, relatively unpolluted runoff from tributary streams.

The wider bends and bays of Nanjemoy feature marshes similar to those seen on Church Creek and Hilltop Fork. Narrower stretches are bordered by a wooded shoreline. These attractive uplands, composed mostly of oaks and pines, always remain in sight to form a pleasant border to the marshland vista.

After about five miles of such enjoyable paddling, you will find that Nanjemoy Creek becomes much narrower, and trees form a canopy overhead. It is possible to paddle to within a short distance of Route 6, a point where the creek is nontidal and choked with logs and downed trees. Return to Friendship Landing by the same route.

Directions

From the Capital Beltway (I-495), take exit 7, Route 5, Branch Avenue, south for 13 miles. Where Route 5 merges with Route 301, continue south for 10 miles to the town of La Plata. In La Plata, turn right on Route 6, go 11 miles, and then turn left on Route 425. Go 2.5 miles, and turn left on Friendship Landing Road. The boat launch is at the end of the road.

From the Baltimore Beltway (I-695), take exit 4, Route 97, south to Route 3, and then to Route 301 to La Plata. From La Plata, follow the above directions.

Other Outdoor Recreational Opportunities Nearby

Mallows Bay with its "ghost fleet" of abandoned ships is about 6 miles away; explore it by canoe or kayak.

GREAT BLUE HERONS

Of the more than 300 species of birds native to Maryland, none is more familiar than the great blue heron. This large wading bird of marshes and rivers is found in every season in every obscure corner of the state. Indeed, the noted environmental writer Tom Horton once suggested replacing the Baltimore oriole with the far more common and easily observed great blue heron as our official state bird. Although awkward and far from handsome, these ungainly birds are somehow undefinably endearing.

Great blue herons stand about four feet tall and have a six-foot wingspan but weigh only five to eight pounds. In large measure, their light weight is due to bones that are hollow, to allow a lighter payload during flight. Herons (and other birds) sometimes have trouble getting airborne after a particularly large meal. Spindly legs and a long thin neck add to the elongate image.

Great blue herons are predators, eating small fish, snakes, frogs, aquatic insects, and soft crabs captured from shallow water and muddy river banks. Far less commonly, and typically during very cold weather or just by accident, herons will take small mammals and insects from adjacent fields. Great blues usually stand immobile, waiting for prey to pass, but they may also stalk slowly through shallow water.

Although herons are familiar to people, their breeding activities are not. They conduct their nesting in private, and relatively few people have visited a breeding colony. Such rookeries are scattered around tributaries of the Chesapeake Bay, where food is plentiful, often with both tidal and nontidal waters nearby. Perhaps the best-known breeding colony was once on the headwaters of Nanjemoy Creek in Charles County; there were almost a thousand nests at this location. However, as the trees died (possibly due to an accumulation of bird guano), the herons abandoned this site, and now most rookeries around the Bay are much less concentrated, averaging less than two dozen nests. Great blue herons begin nesting early in the year, arriving at the nest site reliably within a few days of Valentine's Day. Males claim old nests, the dominant individuals getting the most stable ones. At first, they may fight off the amorous advances of females, but eventually a pair bond is formed. Mating occurs, between one and six (typically three) eggs are laid, and both parents incubate the eggs for about 28 days.

When the eggs hatch, the heronry becomes a chaotic place. The young must be fed regularly, and as soon as one parent gets back to the nest with a full crop, the other leaves. Because nests are close together and landing herons are such large and clumsy animals, territories are vigorously defended with posturing and squawking. Feeding is by regurgitation. Young herons fledge after about two months on the nest. They disperse but are sometimes accompanied and fed by a parent as they learn to hunt. Despite this practice, mortality is high during this "early adolescent" stage.

The period between hatching and fledging is a time when the colony is easily disturbed by visitation. The young sometimes become agitated; if they fall from the nest, they invariably die. Fortunately for the survival of the birds, the ground below a heronry reeks with detritus from the colony: rotting fish parts, regurgitant, huge quantities of droppings, and the occasional dead heron. The unique bouquet of this gumbo tends to keep humans at a distance. In fact, trees that support heron nests eventually die of this guanotrophy; the lifetime of a heronry is about thirty years.

Unlike much of our native fauna, great blue herons are doing well despite an ever-expanding human population. Only disruptions to the heronry, by people or by beavers that girdle and kill trees, are significant threats. Hawks, owls, and eagles rarely bother the nests or adults. Given their adaptability, resilience, and cosmopolitan distribution, great blue herons should remain a well-loved and commonplace part of Maryland's natural landscape for some time to come.

Mallows Bay

River Section: Mallows Bay itself
County: Charles
Distance: Variable, but less than 2 miles maximum
Difficulty: Easy. Tidal flatwater
Hazards: Windy weather possible, iron spikes in the water
Tide Information: https://tidesandcurrents.noaa.gov/tide_predictions.html;
select Maryland and scroll to the Liverpool Point station
Highlights: A historic ship graveyard hosting the remains of dozens of
century-old wooden ships
Nearby Canoe/Kayak Rental: None
More Information: Charles County Parks, (301) 932-3470
Street Address: 1440 Wilson Landing Road, Nanjemoy, Maryland 20662
GPS Coordinates: 38.469004, 77.263540 (boat ramp launch site)

Mallows Bay, on the Potomac River south of Washington, DC, is, hands down, the most unusual and interesting destination for a paddling trip in Maryland. This remote location, in one of the most sparsely populated regions of the Free State, boasts a fascinating history that comes alive only with a visit. Indeed, Mallows Bay is on the National Register of Historic Places and has been nominated as a National Marine Sanctuary. And in practical terms, Mallows Bay can only be seen and appreciated from the seat of a canoe or kayak. It is the largest ship graveyard in the northern hemisphere.

As the United States entered into World War I in April 1917, President Woodrow Wilson recognized the need for ships to transport men and materiel across the Atlantic. Accordingly, he ordered one thousand wooden steamships to be built posthaste. Eighty-seven different shipyards received contracts. Each ship was to be 300 feet long and each would cost taxpayers almost a million dollars.

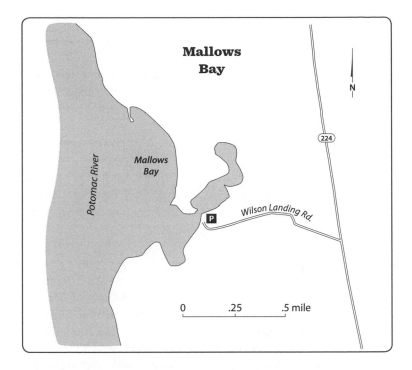

By war's end, only 134 ships had been completed, and 98 delivered. None saw overseas wartime service. Many of the ships were poorly constructed; some leaked and were not even seaworthy. The steel industry that had been built up during the war needed clients, so by 1920 most new ships were constructed of steel, not wood. Additionally, new ships used the recently invented and more efficient diesel engine, rather than the soon-to-be obsolete coal-fired steam engines of Wilson's fleet.

The Navy did not know what to do with those ships on which it had taken delivery. Congress authorized their sale, and in 1922 Western Marine and Salvage Company paid just $750,000 for 233 ships. The ships were moved to a site on the Virginia side of the Potomac River, and salvage operations began. WMSC then bought 566 acres across the river in Mallows Bay and moved the ships there. In 1925, the ships were burned to the waterline, the old hulks settling into the muddy shallows of Mallows Bay.

WMSC never made a profit salvaging the ships of Mallows Bay and went bankrupt early in the Great Depression. The so-called "ghost fleet" sat mostly forgotten for the next decade. During World War II, the demand for scrap iron caused Bethlehem Steel to purchase salvage rights, but again they could not make a profit. After the war, the fleet languished in place for decades. Nature took over; plants began to grow in pockets of soil trapped between ship timbers. The plants grew tall enough to disguise the remaining timbers of most of the ships. Eventually, Mallows Bay came to look like an archipelago of marshland vegetation. Only from the air or by close inspection by boat could the outline of ships be discerned.

An archaeological study in the mid-1990s identified 88 wooden ships, 12 barges, several old workboats, a car ferry, and even a Revolutionary War–era long boat. Only the car ferry is still recognizable today as a ship.

Trip Description

Begin your trip at Mallows Bay Park, owned by Charles County. There is a large unshaded parking lot, portable toilets, and a small fishing pier, but no drinking water or other amenities. Recognizing the popularity of using recreational kayaks to explore the old wrecks, the county has provided a useful polyethylene kayak cradle to assist with launching and landing. Merely put your kayak in the cradle, hop in, and use the handrails on either side to pull you and your boat into the water.

Paddle out into the wide expanse of Mallows Bay. Many of the old wrecks are near the shore; paddle in the direction of anything that looks like an island of vegetation. By staying near shore, you'll avoid the worst of any waves that might arise on a windy day.

The plants that grow on the ship islands are typical freshwater wetland plants, including smartweeds, crimson-eyed rose mallows, tickseed sunflowers, high tide bush, and even a few young trees like sycamores, willows, red maples, and sweetgums. These plants often form long lines perpendicular to the shore, corresponding to the gunwales of the vessel. Look closely near the waterline, and instead of soil you'll see old ships' timbers, twisted with age and often charred.

Wooden ships were held together with iron spikes more than a foot in length, about an inch in diameter, and with a two-inch wide head. Judging by the distance between these spikes, less than two

feet, a wooden ship required a large number of them. And unlike the wood, these iron spikes are still around, albeit rusted. What that means is that the waters of Mallows Bay are studded with projecting spikes, both above and below the water. Use care as you navigate so that your canoe or kayak does not get stuck atop a spike. Make sure the wind does not blow your boat onto a nest of spikes lurking just below the water. Because of these spikes, Mallows Bay is the worst place on the Chesapeake to swim. Inflatable kayaks should not be used here.

A few more tips for paddling at Mallows Bay. You'll be able to see more at low tide, so go at that time if possible. Water clarity will be better after a dry spell, particularly in colder weather when the chill kills off the single-celled algae suspended in the Potomac's waters. Finally, don't forget this little bay has lots of bird life, including bald eagles, great blue herons, osprey, double-crested cormorants, gulls, terns, and ducks.

Directions

From the Washington, DC, Beltway (I-495/I-95), take exit 3, Indian Head Highway, Route 210, south for 18 miles. Turn left on Route 225.

Go 1.5 miles and turn right on Route 224. Go 12 miles and turn right into the park, which is marked by a small sign.

From Baltimore, take either I-95 or I-295 to the Washington, DC, Beltway (I-495) and then follow the above directions.

Other Outdoor Recreational Opportunities Nearby

Nanjemoy Creek is another fine destination for flatwater paddling and is located about a 15-minute drive away.

EELGRASS, SUBMERGED AQUATIC VEGETATION, AND WATER QUALITY

Eelgrass (*Zostera maritima*) is one of the most important life forms to the ecology and biological diversity of Chesapeake Bay. Yet relatively few people have actually seen this flowering plant living in its natural habitat, because eelgrass grows underwater in the shallows of the Bay estuary. If people can recognize this plant at all, it is as the long, slender, blackish green dead leaves that wash up in windrows along the shore or serve as a common packaging material for soft crabs.

Eelgrass grows on sandy to somewhat muddy bottom sediments in the saline waters of the lower Chesapeake Bay at depths of up to nine feet. It requires good water quality, so that sunlight can penetrate through the water to reach the photosynthetic apparatus in the ribbonlike leaf. Once established, eelgrass forms extensive, dense stands known as seagrass meadows. The protection and food provided by these underwater "forests" make them home to an incredible diversity of animals, a unique assemblage of life found nowhere else in Chesapeake Bay.

Few animals directly eat the leaves of eelgrass. However, their surface is colonized by algae, protozoans, and bacteria in high densities. These microscopic plants and animals are grazed upon by worms, sea slugs, and snails; in fact, a typical eelgrass leaf may be covered with so much life that the plant itself may not be visible. The sediments around the bases of eelgrass provide protected homes for more worms, amphipods, clams, and scallops. Developing larval stages of many aquatic animals, as well as fish and crabs, shelter in the waving strands. Indeed, blue crabs in the process of shedding their shells typically make for these safe havens. The leaves, seeds, and roots of eelgrass are eaten by almost two dozen species of waterfowl. The plant removes nutrients like nitrates, present in the Bay in excessive amounts, for use in growth. Finally, the waving beds of dense leaves trap sediments, removing them from the water column. Thus, eelgrass is what ecologists call a keystone species: like the keystone of an arch, it has an importance to the whole community greater than its mere size or abundance would indicate.

Eelgrass and several other species of underwater plants more common in low-salinity portions of Chesapeake Bay are together known as submerged aquatic vegetation, or SAVs—and SAVs are in trouble in the Bay. Massive die-offs of SAVs were noted in the 1970s; by 1984 they grew over only 37,000 acres of bay bottom out of a historic coverage of about 600,000 acres. All the other life dependent on seagrass beds declined correspondingly.

What caused these die-offs of eelgrass and other SAVs? It took scientists several years to unravel the mystery. It is now believed that steadily increasing inputs of nitrogen and phosphorus from sewage treatment plant effluents, agricultural runoff, and atmospheric deposition of automobile exhaust fumes are responsible. These nutrients fertilize the Bay waters, stimulating excess growth of microscopic algae, thereby clouding the water and sheathing the leaves of SAVs so heavily that they cannot conduct photosynthesis. Sediment pollution from eroding construction sites and agricultural lands further exacerbates the problem.

Recognition of what caused the decline of SAVs gave scientists and managers the knowledge with which to design a program to restore Chesapeake Bay. Since 1984 significant and expensive efforts to control the input of nitrogen and phosphorus have been undertaken. The handling of phosphorus has been a success story, in part because it is easier to control and remove than nitrogen, and not inconsequentially because of a ban on

(continued)

phosphate-containing detergents. Nitrogen removal has proven more intractable, but efforts continue.

Eelgrass and other SAVs are bioindicators of how successful programs to control nutrient inputs have been. The total area covered with SAVs has increased to 91,000 acres (in 2015), about halfway to the ultimate goal of 185,000 acres. However, storm events often knock back SAVs. In 2011, the double whammy of Hurricane Irene and tropical storm Lee had significant effects on grassbeds, which took several years to fully recover. Nevertheless, the health of seagrass meadows is generally (but not rapidly) improving. With any luck, we may yet see a further resurgence of these important underwater grasses and the community of animals that they support.

Baltimore oriole. Many Marylanders long to view this colorful songbird, but it's not as rare as it might seem. Arriving about May 1 each year from their neotropical winter home, orioles frequently nest in tall trees like sycamores and silver maples, adjacent to rivers and streams like the Potomac and Monocacy.

Prothonotary warbler. Prothonotaries are birds of the swamp, and a canoe or kayak is the best way to see them. These brilliantly colored birds with loud songs arrive in Maryland about May 1, setting up housekeeping in tree cavities along streams like the Pocomoke, Dividing Creek, and Nassawango Creek.

Blackwater River. The Blackwater winds through the lonely salt marshes of Maryland's mid-Eastern Shore, where eagles are seen more frequently than other paddlers. Sometimes referred to as "Maryland's Everglades," the tidal marshes of the Eastern Shore exemplified by Blackwater Wildlife Refuge offer a sense of isolation and stark beauty found nowhere else in the state.

Northern water snake. Paddlers can't help but encounter the occasional water snake, especially when climbing out of the boat along rocky shorelines. Although generally harmless and not aggressive, water snakes can deliver a bite when provoked. Water snakes also sun themselves while draped on tree branches overhanging the water, especially on placid Coastal Plain streams. Water snakes are ubiquitous, but especially common in warm weather on Tuckahoe Creek, Corkers Creek, and the Virginia Canal.

Bald eagle (*facing page*). Our national symbol and always a remarkable sighting, bald eagles are now surprisingly common. Look for them perched on dead snags or soaring on high, always over bodies of water. Blackwater National Wildlife Refuge is a great place to see eagles year round; Conowingo Dam hosts many dozen eagles each November.

Monocacy River. Draining the rich agricultural landscape of central Maryland, the Monocacy is a river dominated by civilization, yet set apart. Surrounded by a scrim of forest, this riparian corridor is a fine destination for a day of paddling.

Great blue heron. Our largest and most common wading bird, great blue herons are with us year-round in every corner of the state. They are easily observed as they wait patiently for a fish to swim by, which they grab with a lightning-fast lunge. Even Washington's Anacostia River, often relegated (unfairly) to the lower levels of environmental hell, hosts great blues year-round.

Little blue heron. Smaller than its better known cousin, the great blue, little blues rarely stray far from the saltier water of the lower Chesapeake Bay and coastal embayments behind Assateague Island. Look for little blue herons near Janes Island, especially in late summer.

Turk's cap lily. Many consider Turk's cap lilies to be our most beautiful midsummer wildflower. It's a robust plant, growing up to ten feet high, sometimes with dozens of flowers, and prefers the wet alluvial soils of places best reached by canoe or kayak, like Otter Point Creek.

Columbine (*facing page*). While cultivated varieties are a favorite with gardeners, wild-growing columbines are uncommon, at least east of the Blue Ridge. Check rocky ledges near the Potomac River (Virginia Canal, Paw Paw Bends) and Antietam Creek.

Tickseed sunflower. Freshwater marshes like those along Nanjemoy Creek may be Maryland's most biodiverse habitat. In autumn, many such marshes burst with the bright yellow color of tickseed sunflowers (also known as beggarticks); their seeds fall off easily and readily adhere to clothing.

Gunpowder Delta. Close to Baltimore yet seemingly remote, the Gunpowder Delta hosts extensive marshes and swamp forests that provide paddlers with a sense of seclusion.

Persimmons. While persimmon trees do grow on upland sites, they seem to prefer river banks where there is plenty of sun and water. Their conspicuous orange fruits ripen in October and are delectably edible after first frost. Look for ripe persimmons at the Gunpowder Delta and Otter Point Creek, among other locations.

Kenilworth Aquatic Gardens (*facing page*). Paddling Washington, DC's Anacostia River permits entry to Kenilworth Aquatic Gardens from the water. It's a delightful place at all seasons, with beautiful wetland plants.

Horseshoe crab. These awkward-looking arthropods actually pre-date the Age of Dinosaurs and have remained unchanged for several hundred million years. In May, females lumber ashore to lay eggs on sandy beaches in the lower Chesapeake Bay (like Janes Island), but the epicenter of this breeding activity is on the shores of Delaware Bay near Slaughter Beach.

Cardinal flower (*facing page*). A slash of scarlet in wet places, this midsummer bloomer attracts butterflies and hummingbirds. Paddling venues like the upper Gunpowder River and Mallows Bay host cardinal flowers.

Burnside Bridge. On a warm September day in 1862, hundreds of Americans fought and died on and near this bridge spanning Antietam Creek. Known as Burnside Bridge, it is one of the Civil War's best-known landmarks.

Mattawoman Creek

River Section: Mattingly Park upstream to head of navigation
County: Charles
Distance: About 3 miles one way
Difficulty: Easy except when windy. Tidal flatwater
Hazards: None
Tide Information: https://tidesandcurrents.noaa.gov/tide_predictions.html;
  select Maryland and scroll to the Indian Head station
Highlights: A pristine tidal freshwater marsh with some unique wetland
  plants that is renowned for its trophy bass fishing and anadromous fish
  spawning runs.
Nearby Canoe/Kayak Rental: Atlantic Kayak Company, 108A Mattingly
  Avenue, Indian Head, Maryland 20640, www.atlantickayak.com/kayak
  -rentals.html, (301) 292-6455 (open limited hours)
More Information: Maryland Department of Natural Resources,
  http://dnr.maryland.gov/wildlife/Pages/NaturalAreas/Southern
  /Mattawoman-Creek.aspx, Mattawoman Watershed Society,
  www.mattawomanwatershedsociety.org, (301) 751-9494
Street Address: 105 Mattingly Avenue, Indian Head, Maryland 20640
  (Mattingly Park boat ramp)
GPS Coordinates: 38.590322, 77.160720 (Mattingly Park boat ramp)

Mattawoman Creek and its watershed are at a tipping point. Once known for its water quality, with "near ideal conditions," nutrient levels and sediment pollution have increased since 2000, while summer dissolved oxygen levels have gone down. Prized among fishermen for its vernal runs of anadromous fish like shad, perch, and herring, the creek has witnessed a decline of late in the numbers of these fish and their spawning success, likely due to changes in water chemistry. The Mattawoman was once referred to as "what a restored (Chesapeake) Bay would look like," but development in the watershed seems to have reached the stage where its impacts have become discernible. As an increasingly popular bedroom community for Washington, DC, this area has faced enormous pressure for more and better roads, for upscale home construction on single-family lots, and for attracting companies to new business parks. The question is, is this development compatible with maintaining the river and its water quality in near-pristine condition? Or has it already reached the point of no return, slipping away before we realize what has been lost?

That said, the Mattawoman is still a vital river, bursting with biological diversity and beautiful scenery. The lower, tidal stretches host a world-class largemouth bass fishery, well known regionally and nationally, with tournaments almost every weekend May through September. The list of other fish present in significant numbers is lengthy and includes catfish, carp, sunfish, pickerel, crappie, longnose gar, white and yellow perch, American and hickory shad, and alewife. The tidal marshes bloom all summer and fall, with extensive stands of wild rice, pickerelweed, arrow arum, and tickseed sunflower. Mattawoman Creek is one of just a handful of places around the Bay where sizeable beds of American lotus bloom at midsummer. And paddling a canoe or kayak is the best way to experience this bountiful and still relatively unspoiled tidal river.

Trip Description

Launch your canoe or kayak at Mattingly Park in the town of Indian Head. There are restrooms, picnic tables, trash cans, and even a canoe and kayak rental shop (open limited hours). While Smallwood State Park is another possible launch location, it is the focal point of fishing activity on the creek, with attendant motor noise, boat wakes, and crowds. Upon clearing the docks at Mattingly Park, turn left, upriver. Since there may be motorboat traffic, stay close to the vegetation that marks shallow water; this area is biologically more interesting anyway.

The intertidal zone of freshwater tidal rivers like Mattawoman Creek plays host to two emergent perennial plants: arrow arum and pickerelweed. Both have thick rhizomes embedded in the mud

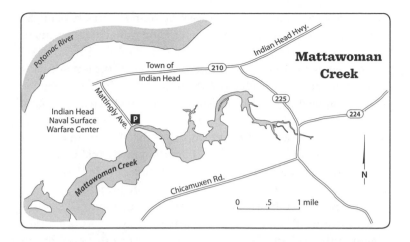

year-round and large tropical-looking leaves that float or are held erect above the water in summer. Flowers, too, are emergent. Pickerelweed has a spike of sky-blue flowers that attract a variety of insect pollinators. Arrow arum flowers are less showy, resembling a pointed rolled leaf (the spathe) surrounding a modest sexual structure (the spadix). It resembles the flower of the familiar terrestrial woodland herb jack-in-the-pulpit; both are members of the arum family, despite growing in remarkably different habitats. The large seeds of both species are important autumn food sources for ducks, although only wood ducks can tolerate the high oxalic acid content of arrow arum seeds.

While arrow arum and pickerelweed are common on every tidal freshwater river in Maryland, another emergent perennial is not: American lotus. Currently found at only four sites in Maryland, American lotus is a spectacular plant, with huge leaves up to several feet in diameter, large, showy cup-like flowers, and seeds that are embedded in a unique structure that resembles an old-fashioned showerhead. Several acres of American lotus form an aquatic garden less than a half mile's paddle upstream of Mattingly Park. Poke the bow of your boat right up into the plants for a good look.

Near the upstream end of the extensive American lotus beds is a small island, the only good spot on this paddle to get out and stretch your legs. There is a bit of shade, and the ten-foot elevation on this ground gives an opportunity to look out over the marshes. If you've brought binoculars, you should see red-winged blackbirds, great blue herons, and Canada geese year-round, a variety of ducks in autumn, and in summer the elusive King rail, which breeds in these marshes.

Proceeding upriver, Mattawoman eventually turns left and runs along a hillside where cyclists on the Indian Head Rail Trail can be seen looking back at you, the marshes, and the creek. There are some tall trees here bordering the river, home to Baltimore orioles. Indeed, much of the nontidal swamp forests of the Mattawoman Creek watershed has been designated an "Important Bird Area" by the National Audubon Society for its extensive tracts of unbroken forest, home to a variety of forest interior-dwelling songbirds.

Within a few hundred more yards, Mattawoman Creek approaches the head of tide, marked by a line of trees. There is a choice of at least three channels you can take in an effort to get as far upstream as possible, but downed trees soon block further progress; I've never made it as far as Route 225, Hawthorne Road, even in spring. The wet forest is still a lovely place, however, with red maples shading grassy banks studded with vernal wildflowers like violets, spring beauties, and meadow rue. When you've explored all of the Mattawoman delta you care to, paddle back downriver toward Mattingly Park.

Along the way, you may note a feathery, yellow, very tall plant farther back in the marsh, behind the line of pickerelweed, arrow arum, and American lotus. This is wild rice, and there are extensive beds of this wetland grass in Mattawoman Creek. An annual, wild rice germinates from seed in May, and within two months the plant may be up to a dozen feet in height. Pistillate (female) flowers top the stalk, where their chances of encountering wind-borne pollen are greatest. Staminate (male) flowers dangle a bit lower on the stem, dispersing their pollen into the air when mature. The seed, a result of fertilization of the pistillate flowers by pollen, ripens in late August. Unfortunately for us humans, red-winged blackbirds savor the immature seeds, so relatively few reach the harvestable stage so familiar in a variety of culinary dishes.

The freshwater marshes of Mattawoman Creek are at their most scenic and interesting in July, August, and September. For the other months of the year, the emergent vegetation dies back, leaving unattractive exposed mud flats.

Directions

From the Washington, DC, Beltway (I-495), take exit 3, Indian Head Highway, Route 210, south. Go 20 miles. Just before Route 210 ends at the Indian Head Naval Surface Warfare Center, turn left on Mattingly Avenue. Go to the boat ramp at the end.

From Baltimore, take I-95 or I-295 south to the Washington Beltway (I-495) and follow the above directions.

Other Outdoor Recreational Opportunities Nearby

Walkers and cyclists will enjoy the Indian Head Trail, whose origin is along Mattingly Avenue between the boat ramp and Route 210.

MANAGING FOR BIODIVERSITY ON PUBLIC LANDS

Preservation of biodiversity is a new paradigm for conservation biology in particular and for science in general, having reached the literature only in the 1980s. Contrary to the paradigms for physics and chemistry, we have so far discovered no universal rules that govern the operation of ecosystems and the direction of the evolutionary process. For this reason, conservation biology is only in its infancy as a predictive science. Increasingly, policymakers want to know how to preserve biodiversity on public lands; science has no certain answers, but a consensus is emerging on a number of management practices that should be successful:

- *Save habitats in large, unbroken tracts.* Island biogeographical theory has clearly demonstrated that the larger a parcel of habitat, the more species it harbors, and that this relationship is synergistic rather than linear.

- *Avoid fragmentation.* Fragmentation creates edge, and edge reduces the effective size of a particular habitat type. A

(continued)

diversity of habitats are acceptable and even desirable at the landscape level, but keep habitat types as unfragmented as possible.

• *Connect these large unbroken tracts with broad habitat corridors.* Greenways of natural habitat promote genetic exchange between populations and promote recolonization in the event of localized extinctions.

• *Preserve areas of critical importance in sustaining biodiversity first.* In the past, public lands have been purchased for their scenic beauty, recreational potential, commercial prospects, or perceived lack of any other value at all. Identify species-rich assemblages, critical habitats, rare communities, and genetically diverse populations through scientific study, and make them the priority for conservation.

• *Limit the influence of human activities on the landscape.* The primary force driving species toward rarity and extinction is the actions of humans. Preserve "hotspots" of biodiversity as reserves closed to the general public except for passive recreation like birding.

• *On lands managed for multiple use, preservation of biodiversity should be the overarching priority and not just a competing use.* When biodiversity is lost from public lands, it will not grow back like trees or return like game animals. Harvesting of plants and animals for commercial gain should take place only on those tracts of public lands not critical for the preservation of biodiversity.

The principles enumerated here may seem extreme, especially to those who are accustomed to utilizing natural resources on public lands rather than conserving them. But the twenty-first century is the first time in history that we have understood the importance of biological diversity for the proper functioning of our biosphere and for the preservation of the raw material of evolution. It is time for a new way of thinking.

Mataponi Creek

River Section: Selby's Landing to head of navigation and return
County: Prince George's
Distance: About 3 miles
Difficulty: Easy, except when windy. Tidal flatwater
Hazards: Windy weather and strong tides possible near the beginning
Tide Information: https://tidesandcurrents.noaa.gov/tide_predictions.html;
    select Maryland and scroll to the Lower Marlboro station
Highlights: A large and biodiverse freshwater marsh that is an important
    stopover site for migrating birds.
Nearby Canoe/Kayak Rental: Patuxent River Park, (301) 627-6074
More Information: Patuxent River Park, Jug Bay Natural Area, http://
    outdoors.pgparks.com/Sites/Jug_Bay_Natural_Area.htm, (301) 627-6074
Street Address: Near 16280 Croom Airport Road, Upper Marlboro, Maryland
    20772 (Selby's Landing)
GPS Coordinates: 38.752569, 76.700017 (Selby's Landing)

The Chesapeake Bay is an endangered estuary, and there's probably not a citizen of Maryland who isn't aware of the situation. From nutrient enrichment to toxic chemicals to habitat loss, each new scientific study seems to send a fresh message of gloom and doom. Oftentimes, however, we forget that the Chesapeake is still a vital and enchanting place. Mataponi Creek, a small tributary of the Patuxent River, is evidence that such special places still exist and that they can be preserved if we have the foresight, leadership, and force of will to do so. Mataponi is a symbol of all that is right with the Chesapeake.

Mataponi Creek is a short, tidal arm of the Patuxent, located about halfway up the watershed in lower Prince George's County. It is protected for much of its length by Patuxent River Park (managed by the Maryland-National Capital Park and Planning Commission) and Merkle Wildlife Sanctuary (managed by the Maryland Department of Natural Resources). Land for Patuxent River Park was acquired in the 1960s when this portion of the county was still quite rural. Each year sees more houses built and more strip developments established; the area is swiftly becoming a bedroom community of Washington, DC.

The Patuxent River is the only major river in Maryland contained entirely within the state. As such, it is a microcosm of the Chesapeake Bay. Its headwaters drain the fast-developing Baltimore-Washington corridor around Columbia in Howard County. Two major reservoirs check its flow almost as soon as it is wide enough to be paddled. Below the dams, the Patuxent's waters enter the Coastal Plain, where tangled swamps with downed trees, infrequent water releases from upstream dams, and restricted lands at Fort Meade and the Patuxent Research Refuge all conspire to keep the paddler at bay. The river becomes tidal near the town of Upper Marlboro and is flanked by wide marshes. At this point, the Patuxent becomes interesting and easily accessible by canoe and kayak.

Trip Description

This trip begins with a recommended visit to the office and visitor center of Patuxent River Park. The naturalists on duty here are friendly and a great source of information regarding almost anything you're likely to see. An observation tower, rebuilt in 2016, gives a panoramic view of the river, which has widened into an extensive marsh known as Jug Bay. Paddlers who rent canoes or kayaks from the park must launch at the boat ramp just down the hill from the park office, known as Jackson's Landing. However, if you have your own boat, a better choice is Selby's Landing, located two miles downstream. Selby's opens up the more intimate Mataponi Creek and shortens the trip to a more manageable distance for novice paddlers. Of course, if you have all day and really want to stretch it out, launch at Jackson's Landing here by the park office. This description is based on a launch from Selby's Landing.

To reach Selby's Landing, leave the park the way you came in. At the park entrance on Croom Airport Road, turn left and drive about two miles to the site of the old airport, now a group camp for Patuxent

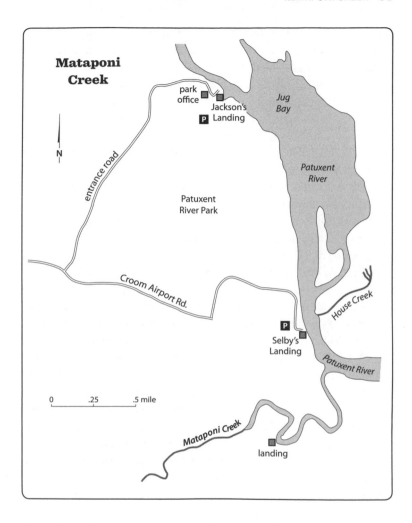

River Park. Turn left again and follow the road to the parking lot for Selby's Landing. There are parking places for about forty cars and a portable restroom here, but no other facilities.

Begin your paddling trip from the boat ramp, heading toward the far side of the river and just slightly upstream. Enter the narrow opening of House Creek. This tiny slough offers an intimate and worthwhile look at the life of a marsh. Tall herbs like cattail, Walter's millet, and swamp loosestrife tower overhead, while tearthumb, smartweed, jewelweed, tickseed sunflower, and marsh ferns occupy a lower layer in between. Making a living among this vegetable diversity are all sorts of insects and spiders, who may drop into your boat as House Creek narrows to just few feet in width. When the going gets too tangled, paddle backwards until you can turn around. House Creek is only a few hundred yards long, but it is lovely and enjoyable.

At the Patuxent River, turn downstream (to the left). This is a good place to look for the large, conspicuous birds of the Patuxent: turkey vulture, osprey, red-tailed hawk, great blue heron, bald eagle, and several types of gulls. Paddlers here in the wider sections of the Patuxent are subject to winds on blustery days that can make the going difficult. Fortunately, you'll be in this exposed area for only about a quarter of a mile.

About 300 yards below Selby's Landing, turn right into the mouth of Mataponi Creek. If the tide is going out, its force can be quite strong here at the junction of Mataponi and the main Patuxent. Within a few hundred yards upstream, however, the tidal bore seems to slacken off, and paddling becomes much easier.

In summer, tall ranks of vegetation close in on both shores of Mataponi. Beyond the front row of lotuslike spatterdock, the common reed (also frequently known by its Latin generic name, *Phragmites*) dominates the right bank. A plant of worldwide distribution, common reed spreads aggressively, especially on sites where the marsh has been disturbed. Reaching heights of up to 12 feet, it has low value as a food source for wildlife but is effective in controlling erosion. The left bank, in contrast, is dominated by wild rice, a high-value food source for many resident and migratory marsh birds. Unfortunately, these birds typically strip the plants of rice grains while they are still immature, so that we humans have to buy our wild rice at the grocery store. The feathery inflorescence, or flower spike, rises high above the rest of the vegetation.

As you paddle farther up Mataponi, two species of flowers that are extraordinarily pretty appear in large numbers. In July, swamp rose mallow, a hibiscus-like flower with huge white petals, studs the marsh. Relatives of the more famous marshmallow, from which colonists extracted the mucilaginous treat of the same name, swamp rose mallows attract hordes of pollinating insects. The fruit, a dried capsule, extrudes brown, shiny seeds. By late summer, the swamp rose mallows have died back, and tickseed sunflower takes over. Growing in rows just behind the spatterdock, the brilliant yellow flowers of *Bidens laevis* make a spectacular show in September.

A half mile or so up Mataponi is a small landing with picnic tables, a portable toilet, and plenty of space. A dirt road leads to an upland area, part of the Merkle Wildlife Sanctuary, and features lots of summer and fall wildflowers. The scrubby habitat here is also well suited for birding.

Continued paddling upriver brings the shoreline trees closer as the marsh narrows. Several interesting marshland shrubs grow at edges where the junction between water and land is sharply defined. Arrowwood has elliptical, widely toothed leaves with unusual blue fruits. Alders have similarly shaped leaves but with flowers that look like small cones. Male flowers are long and thin, giving off a yellow pollen as early as February. Female flowers harden into rounded, woody cones that resemble tiny editions of those on pine trees. Buttonbush has striking white flowers in fuzzy, ball-shaped heads. Winterberry, a member of the same genus as American holly, produces showy, bright red berries in autumn that may persist well into winter if not eaten by birds. All these shrubs are common along the wooded banks of Mataponi.

As the creek narrows, a wooden road bridge crosses it, connecting the two sanctuaries. The bridge, a part of the Critical Areas Driving Tour, is open to vehicles on Sundays only, year-round. Just beyond the bridge, in the middle of the marsh, is a nesting platform for osprey. Such platforms have helped reestablish this large, graceful fish hawk. Decimated by the pesticide DDT in the 1950s and 1960s, populations have rebounded to the point that ospreys are now common in the Chesapeake region.

Within a hundred yards of the upstream side of the bridge, Mataponi narrows quickly to less than a canoe width. Strangely, the sound of rapids is soon heard on this, a tidal creek. The final bend yields the answer to this mystery: beavers have dammed the stream. At low tide, the pile of logs and branches is over a foot high. The beaver dam has raised the water table here in the marsh, flooding areas that previously were wet only occasionally. The result is that all the trees sparsely dotting the marsh have died, leaving only skeletal remains outlined against the sky.

Most paddlers turn around here, but anyone willing to brave a portage through knee-deep mud and thorny vegetation can squeeze out a few hundred feet more of paddling. When you can't go any farther, return to Selby's Landing by the same route.

Directions

From Washington, DC, or Baltimore, take Route 3/301 south beyond Upper Marlboro. Turn left onto the well-marked Croom Station Road. Go 1.6 miles and turn left onto Croom Road. After another 1.6 miles, turn left again onto Croom Airport Road. Go 2.1 miles to the park entrance, passing through (not surprisingly) Croom, Maryland. The park office is another 1.6 miles ahead, at the end of the road.

Other Outdoor Recreational Opportunities Nearby

Several walking and hiking trails exist in Patuxent River Park. Perhaps the nicest is the Black Walnut Nature Study Trail, originating from the park office. Here a boardwalk leads through the heart of some small wetlands, giving you a dry-shod and close-up view of what you had seen previously from the canoe or kayak. For the more serious hiker, a network of trails honeycombs the 600-acre park. Organized groups can make reservations for camping, canoe rental, or a natural history tour in a motor-driven pontoon boat.

COLD GREEN FIRE

Evening settles gently on the creek, and in the gloaming we paddle for home. The day's breeze has died; the water's surface shines as black as liquid obsidian. Silence pervades. At times like this, conversation is superfluous, and even the splash of a careless paddle seems almost a violation of the mood. We head for the light at the end of the dock, then scrape the canoes ashore onto the sand of the adjacent beach.

I step out into the shallows, and I am surprised by a flash of green light. It lingers for less than a second, then fades, an event so evanescent I wonder if I am imagining it. But no: someone's paddlestroke creates a swirling vortex of the same green light. As we haul the canoes up the bank, bilgewater spills out like phosphorescent paint. We are enchanted; what could cause this phenomenon, so strange and ephemeral?

The next morning, a few hours in the library reveals the answer. The light is bioluminescence, released by a marine protozoa called *Noctiluca scintillans*. *Noctiluca* is a common organism with a worldwide distribution, favoring shallow saline and brackish water found along coasts and in estuaries like Chesapeake Bay. It feeds on algae, diatoms, bacteria, and other planktonic organisms, engulfing them, sealing them off inside a membrane, then digesting them. Or rather, most but not all of those algae; a few are stored for later digestion, and it is the chlorophyll of these sequestered algae that gives the emitted light its eerie green cast.

The biochemical reaction that yields light is well studied and is found in a wide variety of organisms. For example, the flash of a firefly is powered by this same enzymatic reaction. The enzyme is called luciferase. When this enzyme encounters a chlorophyll breakdown product called luciferin, the biochemical reaction releases energy as light (most enzymatic reactions release energy as heat). The light lasts for only less than a second, typically in response to mechanical disturbance. Scientists believe the sudden flash of light limits predation; a predator may be so startled by the flash that he releases *Noctiluca*.

Noctiluca is always present in Chesapeake Bay waters, but only reaches the high concentrations that make its presence notable in late summer and early autumn. Bioluminescence is more frequently seen at other, more tropical locales around the globe; several bays in Puerto Rico are well known for this phenomenon.

Evening gives way to full dark, and we stumble up to the campsite. A scatter of stars are bright overhead, but it is the recollection of that cold green fire in the water, flashing like aquatic starshine, that lingers in memory.

Anacostia River

River Section: Bladensburg Waterfront Park downstream and return
County: Washington, DC
Distance: 10.3 miles as described
Difficulty: Easy. Tidal flatwater
Hazards: Wind, tide, occasionally poor water quality
Tide Information: https://tidesandcurrents.noaa.gov/tide_predictions.html;
select Maryland and scroll to the Bladensburg station
Highlights: A surprisingly pretty urban paddling trip featuring a restored
freshwater marsh, with stops to explore Kenilworth Aquatic Gardens and
the National Arboretum
Nearby Canoe/Kayak Rental: Bladensburg Waterfront Park, (301) 779-0371
More Information: Bladensburg Waterfront Park, http://outdoors.pgparks
.com/Sites/Bladensburg_Waterfront_Park.htm, (301) 779-0371;
Anacostia Watershed Society, www.anacostiaws.org, (301) 699-6204
Street Address: 4601 Annapolis Road, Bladensburg, Maryland 20710
GPS Coordinates: 38.933981, 76.9380111 (Bladensburg Waterfront Park
launch site)

Some people look at a river like the Anacostia and see trash, poor water quality, algal blooms, and eroded shorelines choked with invasive, non-native plants. Other people look at the same river and see . . . possibilities. Such folk have a vision for the Anacostia, a vision that includes clean, swimmable, and fishable water a decade from now, a river that is a focal point for the surrounding communities rather than a forgotten backyard, a place to treasure and enjoy rather than a spot to dump trash. Some people continue to write off the Anacostia and say those visionaries are the sort who tilt at windmills. And yet, when paddling the Anacostia on a beautiful autumn day, the trees bursting with color, ducks puddling about in the shallows,

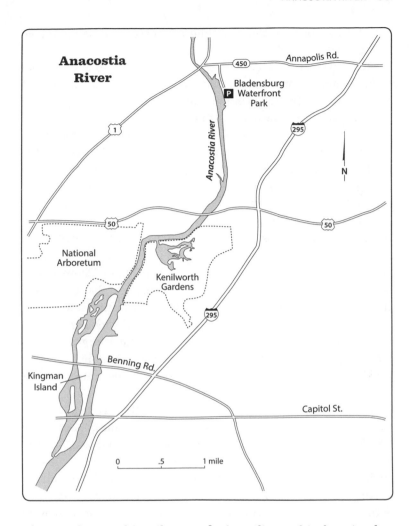

a beaver slapping his tail at you for intruding on his domain, that vision seems like it might actually be possible. It will take hard and continuing work to change the hearts and minds of the citizens who live in the Anacostia watershed, but it is good, honest work, a task worth doing, sustained by a vision worth affirming.

So if you are one of those visionaries, or just someone who would like a glimpse of that vision, go paddle the Anacostia. I guarantee that you'll be surprised—surprised by the scenery, wilder and more beautiful than you imagined, surprised by the wildlife, more common and diverse than you expected, and surprised by the possibilities for a cleaner, healthier Anacostia and the region we live in together.

The Anacostia watershed includes large portions of Prince George's and Montgomery Counties in Maryland and about half of Washington, DC. The United States Capitol, for example, is in the Anacostia watershed. Close to a million people live in the 176-square-mile watershed, and millions more visit and work there. Each one of those people has an effect on the Anacostia: every time a discarded piece of trash blows out of a garbage can, every time a car exhausts hydrocarbons into the air, every time a toilet gets flushed. That's the reason why the District has placed a fee on every plastic grocery bag, is spending millions to create bike friendly commuter routes (like the Anacostia Riverwalk Trail, located adjacent to the Anacostia River), and is upgrading both its ancient sewer system and its modern sewage treatment plant at Blue Plains. These may be small steps, to be sure, but each step is one more in the right direction, and enough steps will eventually reach the destination.

An ideal way to experience the Anacostia is by canoe or kayak. A small boat on the water, powered by your own muscle, gives a connection to this or any river that is visceral and sensory in a way that walking the shoreline or cycling the trail is but a pale imitation. That said, a few caveats are in order.

First, try to paddle the Anacostia on a rising tide. High tide opens up possibilities for paddling that are just not feasible at or near low tide. Three parts of the route described below are impossible to access at low tide. Avoid the worst-case scenario: you paddle into a very shallow wetland with just enough water to float your boat and the sinking tide soon leaves you high and dry. You have only two choices, both bad: wait several hours for the tide to rise again; or try to walk your boat to open water through knee-deep sucking mud.

Second, the Anacostia is polluted by sewage overflows. Contact with the water is not just unpleasant but can be dangerous when bacterial levels are high. For the most part, this situation occurs after heavy rains. For this reason, I recommend paddling the Anacostia only during a prolonged dry spell, typically late summer and fall. A canoe is a better choice than a kayak; at each kayak paddle stroke, water runs down the shaft and onto your hands or into your lap. You probably won't die from Anacostia River water, but it might be wise to carry antibacterial hand wipes to use before your lunch break.

Trip Description

Begin your Anacostia sojourn at Bladensburg Waterfront Park, where you will find ample parking, restrooms, drinking water, small boat rental (including canoes, kayaks, and rowboats), and tide information. Several high schools and colleges base their rowing activities out of this park, and it can be a busy place, with buses unloading and eight- person sculls launching from the docks. Most of the time, however, the waterfront is a quiet place. Launch your canoe from one of the floating docks; kayakers may prefer to use the handy cradles, ideal for such craft.

This area has been a harbor for three hundred years. What is astonishing is that in the colonial era, the water was forty feet deep here and oceangoing ships visited the port of Bladensburg. As land was cleared for farming, erosion brought soil downstream; upon reaching tidewater, it dropped out of suspension. The harbor soon silted up, and Bladensburg lost its role as a center of commerce.

The area nearby was also the site of the 1814 Battle of Bladensburg, in which British troops routed the American militia, subsequently entered Washington, DC, and then burned the Capitol and several other government buildings. Bladensburg is substantially quieter today.

After launching, paddle downriver, to the left. While it is possible to go a few hundred yards in an upstream direction, the fall line is soon reached at a small rapid, and further progress is not possible. The river in front of the docks gets very shallow at low tide and is a favorite loafing spot for gulls and Canada geese.

After paddling about a half mile downriver, look for a side stream entering the Anacostia from your right. As long as the tide is not too low, paddle up into this narrow creek for an intimate look at an Anacostia marsh. Cattails dominate the vegetation, but there are some native grasses, invasive *Phragmites*, and wildflowers like jewelweed and tickseed sunflower. It's a pleasant place, and there is even a small dock with a picnic table far back in the marsh. When further progress is no longer possible, return the quarter mile back to the Anacostia.

Within a short distance downriver, pass under busy Route 50, New York Avenue. The adjacent railroad bridge exhibits an interesting phenomenon that can be seen only from the river. The bridge supports are so old that calcium carbonate has begun to precipitate out of the cement and to drip like stone icicles, or stalactites, analogous to those in limestone caverns.

Two miles downriver from Bladensburg, look for an opening along the left shore, marked by a red-orange bridge of the Anacostia Riverwalk multi-use recreational trail. Paddle under the bridge into a large marsh, part of Kenilworth Aquatic Gardens. Once again, low tide will make significant inroads difficult, but at high tide quite a bit of progress can be made in an upstream direction. Wire cages enclose planted wetland vegetation like arrow arum and pickerelweed; water lilies grow in the open water in summer. This is perfect habitat for turtles, and expect to see several different kinds in warm weather. Finally, the area under the bridge is a favorite hangout for the local beaver; the recently planted trees on the Anacostia Riverwalk Trail here are all protected by wire mesh. It's hard to believe that beavers can live in a river as degraded as the Anacostia, but these aquatic mammals are actually common and thriving here.

Another mile of paddling brings you to the grounds of the National Arboretum, marked by a large sign and a small floating dock suitable for landing. Since this marks almost three miles of paddling, it's a fine location to get out of your boat, stretch cramped legs, and enjoy a snack on the picnic tables. You may enter the Arboretum proper through a gate, open daily 8:30 a.m. to 4:30 p.m., and explore the many wonderful displays of plants on the 444-acre property. The Oriental Collection occupies the hill adjacent to the boat landing, and it is both fascinating and well tended. The National Arboretum is one of the hidden gems of Washington, DC, and is well worth a separate visit at any season.

A pair of bald eagles began nesting on the Arboretum grounds in 2014, and they do most of their fishing in the Anacostia. In spring, when the growing chicks require lots of food, the eagles keep up a steady traffic between their nest on the east side of the Arboretum grounds and the Anacostia River; this is the time of year when you have the best chance of seeing our national symbol as you paddle within the nation's capital. And even if you don't see these eagles while paddling, you can catch them on the internet: the Arboretum maintains a wildly popular live feed video cam, available online, for an even more intimate view into the lives of "Mr. President" and "The First Lady."

Within less than a half mile downstream of the National Arboretum dock, an opening in the shoreline vegetation appears on the right bank, spanned by a wooden footbridge. This marks the northern end of Kingman Island, almost two miles in length. At relatively high tides, paddle under the bridge, watching for errant tee shots from the adjacent Langston Golf Course. The first two hundred yards or so is the most shallow part of this back channel of the Anacostia, so if you can get through here, the rest downstream will be passable.

In contrast to the main river, this slough is bordered by wide freshwater marshes. At any but high tides, extensive mud flats are revealed, attracting scavenging gulls and shorebirds like killdeer. Great blue herons haunt the backwaters, while kingfishers patrol the water with their rattling call. Volunteers have done much good work planting wetland vegetation on these mudflats, judging by the many fenced plots out in the marsh. There is still a fair amount of trash, but otherwise it's hard to believe you are only a few miles from the White House.

Pass under the Benning Road Bridge. Within a few hundred yards is a floating dock attached to a footbridge between the mainland and Kingman Island. This is yet another opportunity to get out of your boat and stretch. A short trail on Heritage Island, to your right, makes for a quick, pleasant walk; there are also trails on Kingman Island, to your left, which are longer but not as scenic.

Back in your boat on the river, pass under the East Capitol Street Bridge; the sweeping roofline of RFK Stadium is on your right. Continue downriver to the south end of Kingman Island. For the 10.3-mile trip described here, turn left into the main Anacostia River, and begin your 5-mile paddle back upriver to Bladensburg Waterfront Park. Alternatively, energetic paddlers may continue a short distance downstream to the well-tended grassy lawns of Anacostia Park, or several miles farther to the trendy scene of the Anacostia Riverwalk, with restaurants, shops, plazas, benches, and other outdoor spaces. Note that below the south end of Kingman Island you'll be sharing the river with large power boats, and the river here is much more open and susceptible to wind.

The paddle back upriver is not as interesting as the downstream trip, with its opportunities to explore obscure backwaters. Nevertheless, a few notable features can be seen. Even on the main river, artificial marshes have been constructed, although they are more industrial than organic. On several inside curves, where rivers tend to deposit rather than scour, solid metal walls have been constructed behind which are marshes of native grasses. Gaps in the metal walls permit the marsh to drain on the outgoing tide, treating paddlers to the incongruous sound of a small waterfall on a tidal river.

Another notable feature of the Anacostia is that a majority of the river's shoreline is reinforced by a seawall just a few feet high, constructed long ago by skilled craftsmen out of native stone. Given the frequent flooding on this urban river, and the twice-daily tides that wash over it, it's surprising these walls still stand.

Approaching Bladensburg Waterfront Park and the end of your trip, it's common to encounter people fishing, either from small rental boats or from the bank. Since the river sediments are polluted with toxins like PCBs, consuming your catch is strongly discouraged. Fortunately, most of these fishers release their catch, being more interested in the sport than in putting food on the table. There are some really big carp in the Anacostia, and in early spring shad still migrate upriver to spawn.

Directions

From either the Baltimore or Washington, DC, Beltways, take I-295, the Baltimore-Washington Parkway, south. Exit at Route 450,

Annapolis Road. Go west on Route 450 for 1.3 miles, then turn left into the well-marked Bladensburg Waterfront Park.

Other Outdoor Recreational Opportunities Nearby

Cyclists and walkers will enjoy the paved, multi-use recreational Anacostia Riverwalk Trail that begins at Bladensburg Waterfront Park and runs downstream. In the opposite direction is the Anacostia Tributary Trail system, with several dozen miles of similarly paved off-road multi-use recreational trails. Greenbelt Park is only about ten minutes away by car and has several good hiking trails within its borders.

RED-WINGED BLACKBIRDS

Every visitor to the marshes of Maryland is familiar with the red-winged blackbird. Males of the species are entirely black except for conspicuous red epaulets on the wings. Females are smaller, with brownish striping over their entire bodies. In winter, red-wings form huge flocks with other blackbird species, roosting in marshes but traveling out to agricultural fields during the day to forage. By spring, these flocks break up, and the birds disperse to marshes across the state to set up breeding territories. In late March, it seems as though even the tiniest patch of roadside wetlands becomes enlivened by red-wing birdsong. Ornithologists believe that red-winged blackbirds are probably the most numerous land birds in the United States, and the same may be true for Maryland as well.

In addition to being abundant and conspicuous, red-winged blackbirds exhibit a complex and easily observed repertoire of behaviors that reflect their mating system and evolutionary success. Red-wings are polygynous; that is, one male mates with more than one female, but a female mates with only a single male. A male red-wing establishes and vigorously defends a territory; each female chooses a territory in which to nest, probably

(continued)

based on the amount of food and other resources available there. The richer the territory, the more females it can accommodate and the more successful they are likely to be in raising young. However, there are trade-offs; a female must decide if she will be better off in a rich territory that may be crowded with other females or in a poorer territory where there is less competition for resources. Availability of resources drives the mating system, but it also has consequences for evolutionary success. The richer the territory, the more dominant a male must be to defend it against all comers. Thus, females tend to mate with the strongest and most dominant males, perpetuating the most vigorous and adaptive traits into future generations.

Male red-wings establish territorial boundaries by singing and displaying their crimson wing patches. Although the territory must be maintained to ensure that enough food is available for the survival of nestlings, time spent in boundary defense is time taken away from foraging. In a polygynous mating system, males must ensure that they eat enough to defend their territories vigorously; in red-wings, males help feed the young and so must devote time to this task as well.

Epaulets are important social signals among red-wings; males use them to indicate their intentions. The entire red patch is exposed when a male is defending territory. Conversely, if a male is searching for an open territory within a colony or wants to forage without attracting attention, he covers the epaulet to signal submission. Although this ploy is not always successful in preventing attacks from birds defending a territory, the severity of the quarrel is reduced when both participants know the outcome in advance.

Lake Roland
and Jones Falls

County: Baltimore

Distance: Section 1: Lake Roland: Up to 3 miles, depending on route
Section 2: Jones Falls: 3.5 miles

Difficulty: Section 1: Easy. Flatwater
Section 2: Mostly easy to moderate whitewater with one Class II rapid

Highlights: Section 1: A thoroughly suburban small lake surrounded by
mature forest and hosting a variety of birds
Section 2: A completely unique urban paddling adventure in a mostly
forgotten river valley with a surprising amount of wildlife

Nearby Canoe/Kayak Rental: None

More Information: http://www.baltimorecountymd.gov/Agencies
/recreation/countyparks/mostpopular/lakeroland/, (410) 887-4156;
Lake Roland Nature Council, www.lakeroland.org, (410) 887-4156

Street Address: Section 1: Near 1000 Lakeside Drive, Baltimore,
Maryland 21210
Section 2: Near 6104 Falls Road (Falls Road Light Rail put-in);
3600 Clipper Mill Road (Meadow Mill take-out)

GPS Coordinates: Section 1: 39.379107, 76.641718
Section 2: 39.376055, 76.650408 (Falls Road Light Rail put-in);
39.330197, 76.642065 (Meadow Mill take-out)

The Jones Falls is one of Maryland's most schizophrenic streams.
Originating from upland springs in the patrician Greenspring
Valley, its upper reaches drain the woods and pastures of the large
horse farms for which that valley is so famous. The narrow little
stream dances over gravelly riffles and through sandy flats, its water
quality protected from the insults that irresistibly accompany

development. Trout lurk furtively in the pools, hiding in the shade of riverbank tree roots. Unfortunately, however, as the Jones Falls nears the Baltimore Beltway, it is joined by side streams that dump in sediment and storm sewer runoff. Downstream of Lake Roland, Interstate 83 occupies the river valley, in places elevated right over the creek. Farther south, in Baltimore City, pollution from industrial waste and broken sewer pipes oozes in, and before long the Jones Falls has been relegated to an urban sewer, running forgotten through the backyards and behind the abandoned factories of Baltimore. As a final insult, the city has enclosed the river in a pipe, and its last two miles flow in stygian darkness under the city and into Baltimore Harbor.

Lake Roland occupies the middle portion of the Jones Falls, where water quality is still decent but will become degraded within a mile downstream. Owned by Baltimore City but located in Baltimore County a short distance north of the city line, Lake Roland was once Baltimore's principal drinking water supply. The old stone dam backs up water for almost a mile. The lake and surrounding greenbelt are a haven for wildlife that finds increasing development reducing its habitat. People visit Lake Roland in surprising numbers, for many of the same reasons. Baltimore County took over management of the park in 2009, has made considerable infrastructure improvements since then, and opened the lake to canoeing and kayaking in 2011.

The Jones Falls downstream of Lake Roland Dam is a truly unique paddling experience, passing through the forgotten heart of north Baltimore. Just a short distance from busy roads and crowded neighborhoods, the Jones Falls Valley harbors an unusual degree of solitude and is a haven for urban wildlife. For one or a few days each year, water is released from Lake Roland and makes a paddling trip on the Jones Falls possible. It's an experience not to be missed. Consult the Lake Roland Nature Council website for more information.

Trip Description

Section 1: Lake Roland

Unload your boat in the small parking lot on the east side of Lake Roland, at the end of Lakeside Drive. Before starting your trip, it's worthwhile to walk back down Lakeside Drive to view the old Lake Roland Dam. This dam was for many years the most dangerous one in Maryland; during Hurricane Agnes in 1972, it came very close to

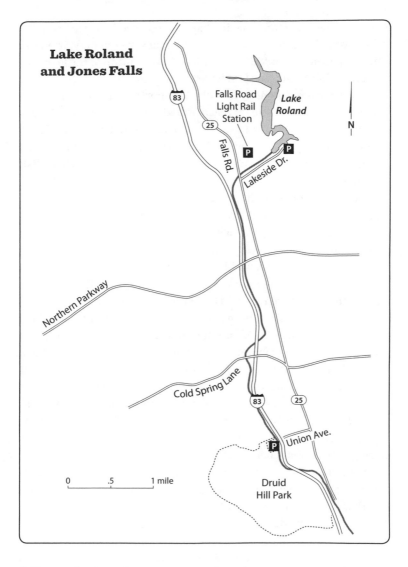

Lake Roland and Jones Falls

Falls Road Light Rail Station

Lake Roland

83

25

N

Falls Rd.

Lakeside Dr.

Northern Parkway

Cold Spring Lane

83   25

Union Ave.

0   .5   1 mile

Druid Hill Park

failing, and evacuations were carried out downstream. It took twenty years for the money to be found to rehabilitate the old dam, despite the obvious danger; fortunately, it held in the interim, and it is now safe. At dawn or dusk in summer, the footbridge is a good place to observe yellow-crowned night herons fishing from the rocks below the dam. Returning to the parking lot for your boat and paddling gear, you'll pass the pump house, built in the Greek Revival style and still an impressive structure even if it hasn't been used in a century. Lake Roland was Baltimore City's first municipal water supply, from the dam's construction in 1860 until 1915, when siltation of the lake prevented further withdrawals of water.

Kayaks are most easily launched by portaging about 50 yards north from the parking lot to reach a shady bankside put-in. Canoes may also be launched here, but can also be lowered over the edge of the pump house's concrete palisade just a few yards from the parking lot. (Getting into and out of a kayak off the edge of this vertical wall is difficult.)

Paddle in a northerly direction, away from the dam. While almost all of Lake Roland is bordered by mature trees, some of the largest are in a shallow cove to your right. Sycamores, American beech, tulip poplars, and a variety of oaks form a dense canopy that abounds with migrating songbirds in early May. By autumn, cooler weather brings out the full spectrum of fall color in these trees; those hues are especially intense when reflected in the dark waters of the lake.

On the opposite shore is one of the park's most familiar sites: Paw Point Dog Park. A membership-only, one-acre fenced enclosure gives dogs the freedom to run and play off-leash, and even swim in Lake Roland. For decades prior to Paw Point's 2011 opening, this area of Lake Roland Park was literally loved to death by dogs and their owners; fecal coliform levels both in the soil and the lake were often at dangerous levels. When the park was refurbished starting in 2009, the offending soil had to be dug up and hauled away as hazardous waste, and the area reclaimed with clean soil from elsewhere.

Paddling around the corner of this peninsula reveals a berm that seemingly blocks further progress. This supports the light rail line that connects downtown Baltimore with its northern suburbs. There's a small bridge that allows you to paddle through the berm and under the railbed; it's noisy and scary if a train passes overhead while you're under the bridge. Look for the nests of barn swallows, half cups of mud cemented to the bridge eaves. Barn swallows are elegant, slim birds with long wings and forked tails, fast and agile fliers with a twittering song.

Ahead lies the largest portion of Lake Roland, an area of open water that attracts Canada geese, gulls, and mallard ducks. It's not uncommon to see a bald eagle here either, attracted by the good fishing in shallow water. Lake Roland supports largemouth bass, catfish, common carp, and sunfish, but a 1986 study found elevated levels of the pesticide chlordane in the flesh of some fish. Consequently, a fish consumption advisory was issued, so Lake Roland fishing is preferable as a catch-and-release venue.

The upper end of Lake Roland is fed by two streams, Roland Run and the Jones Falls, and both can (and should) be explored. Roland Run enters from the north; to find it, look for subtle signs of flowing water among the maze of reeds and shrubs. The channel narrows to less than a canoe width and becomes overhung with trees like silver maple and box elder. After about 100 yards, a shallow gravel bar and some small riffles prevent further progress upstream. Nearby on private land is the L'Hirondelle Club, founded in 1872; members often paddled on Lake Roland in the early decades of the twentieth century, when canoeing was a popular social activity.

Returning to the marshy north end of Lake Roland, look for the entrance to its main feeder stream, the Jones Falls. These wetlands often harbor a good diversity of birds, including great blue herons, kingfishers, and assorted sparrows. During spring and fall migration look for shorebirds on the mud flats, coots and teal on the open water, and various woodpeckers and songbirds in the overhead trees. The Jones Falls is a larger stream than Roland Run, so further paddling progress upstream is possible as long as no downed trees block the way. A popular hiking trail parallels the creek, so there is not a sense of solitude, but the Jones Falls is quite pretty.

Once you've reached the limits of navigability, return to Lake Roland and paddle back to where you put in. Although exact mileage on such a circuitous and random route is not possible, allow about three hours to fully explore all the nooks and crannies of Lake Roland.

Section 2: Jones Falls

The Jones Falls from near the Lake Roland Dam downstream to Meadow Mill may just be the most unique paddling trip in Maryland. For most of the year there's not enough water in the river to float a toy rubber ducky, and when stormwater runoff brings the Jones Falls to paddleable levels, you really don't want to be on the extraordinarily polluted water. But once or a few times a year, water is released from Lake Roland dam, just to make sure the gates and mechanics still function. And this is your opportunity, a chance to paddle a river like no other, on a day with reasonable water quality. But be forewarned:

the Jones Falls has a few locations where the novice paddler could flip over. In places, the current is fast, overhanging vegetation slaps you in the face, and your boat can get hung up on rocks if you don't put it in the correct spot. Most importantly, you need to be able to recognize the take-out location from river level, because if you miss it, you'll be in for a mile of serious rapids that can only be paddled by teams of skilled whitewater paddlers using all safety precautions.

Launch your canoe or kayak from the back side of the Falls Road light rail parking lot. There is ample parking here on weekends, but the lot tends to fill with commuters' vehicles on weekdays. The river soon takes a bend to the left, the current picks up, and you're off to the races. In the next half mile there are few chances to stop; the floodplains that characterize natural rivers have on the Jones Falls been built up with fill and then paved over for parking lots and other development. In places concrete walls rise directly out of the river to support Falls Road and other motorways, and stone-filled wire baskets called gabions retard adjacent eroding slopes. Between Northern Parkway and Cold Spring Lane, the Jones Falls butts up against a vertical concrete wall on the right, atop which is Interstate 83. The sound of traffic is almost deafening, and it's a disconcerting feeling to know a major highway is only a few feet away. Other riverside features that are rarely found on more natural rivers can be seen along the Jones Falls. For example, storm water pipes, some as much as eight feet in diameter, appear from the side; it's easy to imagine the volume of water these pipes dump into the Jones Falls during a major summer thunderstorm.

To keep track of your downstream progress, count the bridges you pass under; there are four. The Falls Road bridge is just below the put-in; the Kelly Avenue Bridge is at mile 0.5, Northern Parkway at mile 1.0, Cold Spring Lane at mile 2.5, and 41st Street at mile 3.0.

Despite the urban character of the Jones Falls, there is a surprising amount of wildlife that an alert paddler might see. Kingfishers, turkey vultures, black vultures, mallards, and great blue herons are common. Yellow-crowned night herons are rare elsewhere in Maryland, but are sometimes seen perched in riverside trees; there is a small nesting colony downstream of the section of river described. Hawks and even the occasional bald eagle soar above the river. Songbirds abound in the brushy areas and in riverbank trees during their spring migrations. Mammals are less commonly seen, but raccoons, opossums, and red foxes have all adapted to the urban environment and seek shelter in the river valley where humans rarely venture. Why this surprising amount of animal life? In the concrete jungles that constitute most of Baltimore, natural areas are few. Even small pockets of habitat and narrow corridors that contain water draw what wildlife there is and tend to concentrate those animals to a density uncommon elsewhere. In addition, Cylburn Arboretum and Druid Hill Park occupy the slopes to the west of the Jones Falls, contributing their acres of natural habitat. The intervening interstate highway and light rail corridor is no problem for vagile animals like birds.

This river contains one rapid of significance. About a quarter mile downstream of Cold Spring Lane, a long section of deep water with a slow current ends in a noisy, rock-strewn drop; pull over on the right several yards in advance, before you get sucked into the rapid unprepared, and scout from shore. The best route is about 5 feet off the right shore, but many paddlers still end up hitting rocks, and upsets are possible, especially for tandem canoes. Fortunately there is a slow-moving pool at the bottom to collect boats, gear, wet paddlers, and bruised egos.

From this point, the take-out is not far away, but the Jones Falls still has a novel feature found on few, if any, other rivers. As the river valley narrows downstream of the 41st Street bridge, Interstate 83 has been constructed directly over top of the Jones Falls. The concrete pillars supporting the roadbed seem like trees in a forest; they form a complex slalom course for canoes and kayaks. The river widens and its speed picks up, making the river shallow and rocky. Good river-reading skills are essential to get through this without scraping, but you may have to get out in the ankle deep water and drag your boat in some sections.

The moment you emerge from under the Jones Falls, paddle to the right shoreline and beach your boat on the cobbles. This is your take-out, which you should have scouted prior to making this run so that you can recognize it from river level. Haul your canoe or kayak through the riverside weeds and trash and over the guardrail into the parking lot of the Meadow Mill complex of buildings.

A note of caution: you MUST be able to recognize this location from the river and take out here. Below this point, the Jones Falls runs through a steep-sided valley for another mile; there is no good way to get out, and the river drops over a series of more difficult rapids. They culminate at the site of an old partially demolished dam where the river drops six vertical feet into a churning cauldron of whitewater that will turn over every canoe and recreational kayak. This is followed by Round Falls, a twelve-foot high wooden dam that when attempted by whitewater kayakers has resulted in a number of painful injuries.

Having successfully exited the river at Meadow Mill, you'll need to get back to your car at the Falls Road light rail station. This is an opportunity for yet another unique feature of this river; catch the light rail from the Woodberry Station, found on the other side of the Meadow Mill complex of buildings. Just make sure you have money for the fare and know the schedule.

Directions

Section 1: From the Baltimore Beltway, take the Falls Road (Route 25) exit. This road heads north only. At the first stoplight, turn left onto Falls Road proper. Go 3.4 miles south, cross the new Falls Road Bridge, and make an immediate left onto Lakeside Drive. Follow Lakeside Drive to the end.

Section 2: To reach the put-in, bear left off Lakeside Drive (see above) at the sign for the Falls Road Light Rail station. To reach the take-out from the Light Rail station, turn left onto Falls Road from Lakeside Drive. Proceed 3.2 miles; turn right on Union Avenue. Go one-third of a mile and turn left on Clipper Mill Road. Drive 100 feet and turn right, crossing a wooden bridge over the Jones Falls into the Meadow Mill complex.

CONSERVATION AND PRESERVATION IN MARYLAND

The fate of publicly owned lands in Maryland depends in large measure on citizen opinion and input. With an ever-expanding human population, we face a future in which such lands will become increasingly more valuable for both aesthetic and economic reasons. The dichotomy between utilization of such lands for resources by logging, mining, trapping, and hunting, and preservation through a ban on such activities, is a tension that can be expected to increase as society debates the question.

We have long recognized that certain locales should be preserved exclusively for nonconsumptive uses. By reason of their scenic beauty or the opportunity they present for recreation, parks and wilderness areas ban the harvesting of minerals, plants, and animals. Such areas are under increasing strain, however; in many places, especially near metropolitan centers, parks are literally being loved to death. Recognizing the value of such lands, the Maryland legislature established Program Open Space, a pool of money derived from a surtax on real estate transfers, to fund future purchases of parklands. Unfortunately, the fund has been diverted in recent years to supplement general state revenues. This action is shortsighted for a number of reasons, but the most obvious one is that land is a finite and increasingly scarce commodity.

The majority of state lands are managed for conservation rather than preservation. Conservation can be broadly defined as the wise use of land and its living resources on a sustainable basis. Although the words sound simple and reasonable, the institution of these concepts is difficult, complex, and subject to widely differing interpretations of such words as wise use and sustainable.

For example, wise use has always implied an economic benefit. Profits from the sale of timber off state lands revert to the state treasury; activities and sales of gear associated with hunting generate economic benefits to the local business community. From this viewpoint, forests are merely tree farms and lands are free-range game ranches. The problem with this belief is that the majority of living organisms have no direct economic value but do play a significant role in maintaining the ecosystem. The entire range of organisms that form the ecological community, especially unobvious or poorly appreciated ones like bacteria, fungi, and insects, provide ecosystem services to us free of charge. They filter pollutants, retard the loss of soil, buffer stream flow, recycle nutrients, purify the air, and stabilize the environment

(continued)

against natural and artificial extremes. Similarly, charismatic organisms like wildflowers and warblers are among the most beautiful inhabitants of forests, but their value, although aesthetically priceless, cannot be quantified.

What our society needs, therefore, in order to decide upon the proper balance between use and preservation of state lands, is a widespread appreciation among citizens of what Aldo Leopold calls a "land ethic." A land ethic changes our role in the ecological community from one of dominance, in which we decide the future and fate of the land and all the species that inhabit it, to one of cooperative equality, in which our actions promote the long-term diversity, complexity, and stability of the natural world. Our relation to the land will now impose obligations as well as confer privileges. We will continue to manage, use, and alter natural resources, but we will also acknowledge our responsibility to do so as a last resort and for the good of all rather than for the self-interest of a few—especially on our public lands.

Our human society operates under such ethics as a matter of course. For example, all taxpayers, even those without school-age children, contribute to the operation of public schools because education is recognized as an important benefit to the society as a whole. A land ethic merely extends such cooperation and mutual respect to include the natural world that we share.

Gunpowder Delta

River Section: Mariner Point Park and environs
Counties: Harford and Baltimore
Distance: 10 miles as described; shorter routes possible
Difficulty: Easy. Tidal flatwater
Hazards: Windy weather possible, powerboat traffic
Tide Information: https://tidesandcurrents.noaa.gov/tide_predictions.html;
   select Maryland and scroll to the Pond Point station
Highlights: A labyrinthine freshwater marsh with forested borders
Nearby Canoe/Kayak Rental: None
More Information: Gunpowder State Park, (410) 592-2897. Mariner Point
   Park, www.harfordcountymd.gov/Facilities/Facility/Details/Mariner
   -Point-Park-69, (410) 612-1608
Street Address: 100 Kearney Drive, Joppa, Maryland 21085 (Mariner
   Point Park)
GPS Coordinates: 39.400573, 76.351273 (Mariner Point Park put-in)

In the seventeenth century, central Maryland was a very different place. Farms carved from the primeval forest grew tobacco, the colonies' single most important crop. The fields were tended by slaves and indentured servants. Roads served only to link backcountry farms to tidewater ports, where hogsheads of tobacco were shipped to the Old World. The colonies were united by their waterways, and nowhere was this more true than in Maryland. The ports of Joppa-towne and Elkridge were preeminent; Baltimore was still a small town, growing in importance only slowly.

Today, the focus of life has changed in many ways. Agriculture is only a minor part of the economy, especially in the heavily populated central part of Maryland. Road and air transportation bring people, goods, and services to other parts of the state. The old colonial ports are no longer bustling centers of commerce; indeed, Elkridge and Joppatowne are no longer served by ships.

No trace of colonial Joppatowne exists; it is now a quiet residential community of neatly kept homes in the best suburban tradition. The reason for this change? The tidal Gunpowder River, once serving Joppatowne's 12-foot-draft ships, has silted in. Extensive islands of sediment, carried downriver by floods and storm events, dot what was once the deep, open water of the Gunpowder Delta. Marshes and wooded swamps cover the islands.

The sources of all this sediment are the two Gunpowder Rivers, the Big and Little, which converge here. The rivers drain much of the northern and eastern parts of Baltimore County and the western part of Harford County; development has made them more susceptible to flooding and the accompanying loss of topsoil. This is not just a recent development; accounts of siltation reach back to the eighteenth century. Indeed, with much of the Big Gunpowder watershed held back by dams, the river's contribution to sediment inflows has been greatly reduced since their construction in the first part of the twentieth century.

All this is good news to canoers and kayakers looking for a place to paddle. The Gunpowder Delta is nearby, especially for Baltimore-area boaters, and surprisingly pristine. The tangle of waterways offers many opportunities for exploration. Although powerboaters, especially fishermen, use these same rivers, there are a few shallow areas where you can experience a sense of isolation and remoteness unusual for a paddling trip so close to civilization.

Trip Description

Put your canoe or kayak into the water at Mariner Point Park in Joppatowne. There is plenty of parking, and trash cans, portable toilets, and a picnic pavilion are available at the park. From the tiny beach designated for canoe/kayak access to the river, paddle downstream (to the left). This body of water is a dredged arm of the river, which provides access to backyard boatslips for upstream residents. For this reason, motorboat traffic is heavy on this part of the river. However, both the traffic and the scenery improve quickly.

The canal dumps you out onto the wide expanses of Bird River. Turn right, staying close to a line of tall reeds. *Phragmites* grows on

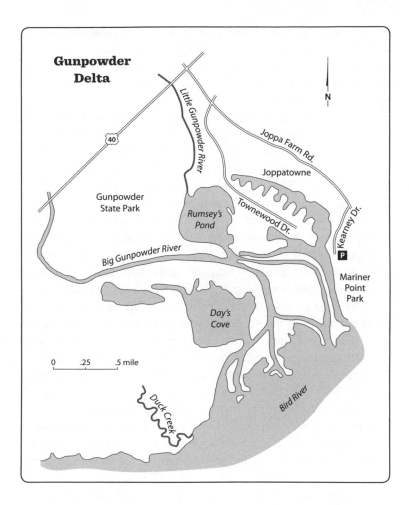

Gunpowder Delta

N

40

Little Gunpowder River

Joppa Farm Rd.

Joppatowne

Gunpowder State Park

Rumsey's Pond

Townewood Dr.

Kearney Dr.

P

Big Gunpowder River

Mariner Point Park

Day's Cove

0   .25   .5 mile

Duck Creek

Bird River

disturbed marsh soil, and here, on the exposed face of the Gunpowder delta, it forms a monoculture, outcompeting every other kind of wetland vegetation. Continue paddling across the face of these marshes, keeping open water and the Amtrak line on your left. After more than a mile and a half, you'll reach the forested mainland.

Just a few hundred yards farther along you will come to an opening in the curtain of marsh grasses. This is Duck Creek, so obscure and tiny that it is not even named on topographic maps. Despite its anonymous nature, Duck Creek is a little aquatic gem. As it winds its way deep into the freshwater marsh for almost a mile, you'll be likely to scare up herons, red-winged blackbirds, beavers, and the creek's namesake ducks. Submerged aquatic vegetation grows so thick in Duck Creek that, by autumn, it forms a mat so dense as to impede your progress upstream. When you reach the head of navigation, lie back in your boat and marvel at how quiet and naturally pristine such a place can be when it is so close to suburbia.

Return to the mouth of Duck Creek, turn left, and follow the wooded shoreline north. The channel becomes narrower; it is actually one of the four mouths of the Big Gunpowder River. At the first opening in the treeline, almost a mile from Duck Creek, paddle left into Day's Cove. This bay, about a half mile in diameter, is very shallow, and this characteristic serves to keep motorboats out and ensure that you'll have the cove all to yourself. Like Duck Creek, Day's Cove is also pristine, the uplands on its east side being protected by Gunpowder State Park and the Eastern Sanitary Landfill. Bald eagles are often sighted here. The state has recently developed this area into an environmental education facility for use by schoolchildren.

Leaving Day's Cove by its only exit, turn left and continue paddling upstream on the Big Gunpowder. The marshes are soon left behind, and the Gunpowder takes on the look of a true river, with well-defined banks thickly forested. When an opening in the trees appears on the right, paddle through it. This channel connects the Little and Big Gunpowders, separated here by only a few feet of intervening forest; continue north on the channel through a chain-link fence that has been mostly torn down. You are now in Rumsey's Pond, a flooded gravel mine only recently opened to boaters. It is one of many active or abandoned gravel mines in the area. Explore the pond as you wish; it is not as large as Day's Cove.

As you exit from Rumsey's Pond, there is a small patch of dry land suitable for lunch, a snack, or a break. From this point, make your first left and paddle downstream on the Little Gunpowder River. Continue down the Little Gunpowder for more than a mile to its junction with Bird River. Bear left and then left again to return to the dredged channel leading to the launch site in Mariner Point Park. If all this sounds confusing, check the map for clarification.

Finally, a note about nomenclature. The Gunpowder is one of the nation's most colorfully named rivers. Local lore has it that when the colonists first arrived, Native Americans were greatly impressed with the noise, smoke, and killing power of the settlers' firearms. Obtaining some gunpowder in trade, they planted it along the banks of the river in hopes that, like corn, it would grow and produce more of itself.

Directions

From Baltimore, take I-95 north. Exit at Route 43 east (White Marsh Boulevard). Turn left onto Route 40 east. After traveling 4.7 miles on Route 40, crossing both Gunpowder rivers, turn right on Joppa Farm Road. Go 1.6 miles and turn right on Kearney Road. Follow Kearney Road to the park entrance.

Other Outdoor Recreational Opportunities Nearby

Otter Point Creek is another fine freshwater marsh suitable for canoeing. It is located about 10 miles northeast of Mariner Point Park.

CHESAPEAKE BAY: ORIGINS

The morning mist curls and boils as it rises from the water; the sun edges above the trees, filling the world with diffuse light. The water is alive with ripples and little splashes, and over by the shore a heron rises, flying off silently on pterodactyl wings. The coolness of dawn lingers on your skin, and the cares of past and future seem irrelevant to the pleasures of today. So it has been on Chesapeake waters for hundreds of years; the timelessness of this experience extends across the generations. For many of us, the Chesapeake Bay is the essence of Maryland, and this emotional attachment has been the driving force in the campaign to "Save the Bay."

Chesapeake Bay, as we know it, has existed for about 12,000 years. Its origins, however, are far older, dating back almost two million years to the time when Pleistocene ice sheets covered much of northern North America. During this ice age, the colder global climate caused a recession of the oceans from the

(continued)

continental land masses as water became tied up in ice. What is now the Susquehanna River drained meltwater from the southern edge of these glaciers, flowed southward in its channel, and emptied into the sea near the point where the continental shelf is now found. Eventually, the climate warmed, ocean levels rose as glacial ice melted, and the sea drowned the lower parts of the Susquehanna. This alternating pattern of cold ice ages and warmer interglacial periods continued for almost two million years. Glaciers advanced three more times; the last ice age ended about 12,000 years ago. Thus humans have populated the Bay area only in the most recent interglacial period, a time when the Atlantic Ocean has flooded the lower reaches of the Susquehanna to create the modern incarnation of Chesapeake Bay. Indeed, if you examine a nautical chart of the Bay, the old riverbed of the Susquehanna is readily apparent as a deep channel. The sea level has risen sufficiently to fill the old riverbed to the top, and then some; water has spread out onto the Susquehanna's floodplain. Thus the Bay is much wider than the historical riverbed.

For this reason, Chesapeake Bay is known as a drowned river estuary. But what is an estuary? Scientists describe it as a semi-enclosed body of water open to the ocean and measurably diluted by fresh water. Chesapeake Bay fits this definition exactly: it is surrounded by land on three sides, but it is open to the Atlantic at its mouth near Cape Charles, and at the opposite end the Susquehanna pours in millions of gallons of fresh water every day, even during the most severe drought. Salt and fresh water mix in a complex fashion and spread out over the shallow pan of the Bay.

Yet as one views the Bay from a small boat in a sheltered cove on a summer morning, its dynamic geology and hydrology pale to insignificance against the sensory attractions of the here and now. For most of us, it is the tug of freedom and changelessness and natural beauty that brings us back time and again to enjoy the simple pleasures of life in the "Land of Pleasant Living."

Otter Point Creek

River Section: Otter Point Landing upstream to head of navigation and return
County: Harford
Distance: 4.0 miles
Difficulty: Easy, except when windy. Tidal flatwater
Hazards: Windy weather possible
Tide Information: https://tidesandcurrents.noaa.gov/tide_predictions.html; select Maryland and scroll to the Pond Point station
Highlights: A beautiful freshwater marsh with a diverse collection of summer wildflowers
Nearby Canoe/Kayak Rental: None
More Information: Anita C. Leight Estuary Center, www.otterpointcreek.org, (410) 612-1688
Street Address: 601 Otter Point Road, Abingdon, Maryland 21009 (Otter Point Landing)
GPS Coordinates: 39.446421, 78.266033 (Otter Point Landing boat ramp)

In the ever-expanding sprawl of development that characterizes the Boston–Washington corridor, a few places get left behind, bypassed by roads, cut off by railroad lines, and encircled by housing tracts. These little backwaters of natural landscape are often pleasant retreats of surprisingly pristine beauty and a haven for wildlife that has been pushed out of surrounding areas. So it is with the region between Baltimore and the head of Chesapeake Bay to the east of old Route 40. Both Otter Point Creek and the Gunpowder Delta (see elsewhere in this book) are pleasant freshwater marshes with forested wetland borders. At the more northeasterly Otter Point Creek, a wide estuary bifurcates into narrow passageways that eventually become closed over by trees. This diversity of scenery makes Otter Point Creek a fine area to explore by canoe or kayak.

Large sections of the upper stretches of Otter Point Creek are protected through an unusual consortium of agencies. The estuary is a component of the Chesapeake Bay National Estuarine Research Reserve, administered by the National Oceanic and Atmospheric Administration (NOAA). Harford County owns a small park, the Anita C. Leight Estuary Center, on the more open part of Otter Point Creek, which has hiking trails through 50 acres or so of hilly upland forest and is used for environmental education. Finally, a large tract of forested wetlands that borders the upper reaches of the creek was the farsighted gift of Melvin Bosley to the Isaac Walton League. This area is known as the Bosley Conservancy, and it has a pleasant but usually muddy trail through a swamp forest with some really big old trees.

Trip Description

Put your canoe or kayak into the water at Otter Point Landing. There is only limited parking here, but a portable restroom has been thoughtfully provided. In the event these few parking spaces are filled, you can always park along Route 40 at what is locally known as "Smith Park"—simply a long pullout along the highway. Access to the water requires a short bushwhack through the vegetation, and at low tide the put-in will be muddy. The Anita C. Leight Estuary Center discourages carrying boats the 500 feet from their parking lot to the water.

You may feel a bit silly launching a small boat among all the cabin cruisers anchored at the adjacent Otter Point yacht club, but they're headed downstream toward the Bush River and Chesapeake Bay, whereas you'll be paddling upstream into the shallows and marshes. Bear right (upstream) from the launch ramp and cross Otter Point Creek, aiming for a wooded knob of land on the far shore. As you go around this corner, the estuary of Otter Point Creek opens to view: a wide, marshy expanse filled with lots of green emergent vegetation.

To the left is a shallow bay (Eagle Cove) that always has several great blue herons. The still, warm waters of this embayment, less than a foot deep, attract all sorts of small and juvenile fish that form the principal prey of these graceful birds. When not actively fishing, the herons congregate in trees along the shore; it is not unusual to have a dozen of them in sight at any one time. Bald eagles may often be seen here as well; Aberdeen Proving Grounds, just downstream on

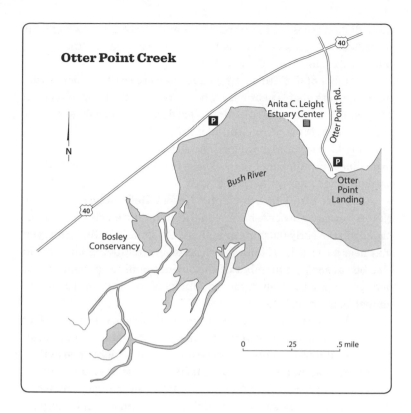

the other side of Bush River, hosts one of the eastern United States' largest concentrations of our national bird.

The far end of the Otter Point Creek estuary is a maze of small channels that twist and turn through beds of spatterdock, arrow arum, pickerelweed, and wild rice. Most of these little coves are blind, so you can't get very far. However, these sloughs are good places to surprise herons, mallards, and wood ducks.

Paddle across the face of the marsh toward a small island of trees located in the center of the bay. This is Snake Island, a privately owned oasis of high ground that is used for environmental education programs run by the Anita C. Leight Estuary Center. This is the only place along the route where you can get out of your boat, stretch, eat a snack, and enjoy some shade on a hot day; be sure to carry out all your trash (and the trash of those less considerate). To continue, paddle down the channel, keeping Snake Island on your right; this leads into the true riverbed of Otter Point Creek and will give you access to the more distant reaches of the stream. Should you be uncertain of your route, look for numbered markers atop posts driven into the marsh; number 7 is found near Snake Island.

A number of mallard nesting structures are scattered across the marsh and are visible near here. These are wire mesh tubes set atop poles and intertwined with compressed foliage to provide shelter from the sun. Most people think of mallards as very common and tame ducks (they are), but North American populations have been in decline for a number of years. These nesting structures help deter predators and increase hatching rates.

Are there otters in Otter Point Creek? Definitely: staff at the NOAA Research Reserve have seen these shy and elusive mammals, usually in the early morning or at dusk. On some paddling trips, you may hear an occasional loud splash, as of an otter diving, but it could also be caused by a member of the several families of beaver that occupy the marsh. Count yourself lucky if you are ever fortunate enough to see river otters.

Much of the vegetation lining Otter Point Creek is five or six feet high, cutting off long views over the marsh. Cattails are common, although, as the creek approaches the upland areas, richer and better-drained soils allow herbaceous plants like Joe-Pye weed, smartweed, Turk's cap lily, sneezeweed, and other late-summer composites to grow. Eventually, small trees like red maple and box elder appear along the shores, and soon the open expanse of marshland gives way to wooded swamp.

Otter Point Creek narrows and becomes shallow as the canopy closes overhead. The impression is that of paddling through a green tunnel. Some of the trees are very large, and this swamp harbors a number of songbirds, judging by the evening chorus. Peepers and other frogs abound in spring; plagues of deerflies sometimes come out in June. Several persimmon trees hang over the water, allowing the paddler to enjoy a healthy wild snack without leaving the boat. Be aware, however, that persimmons require a good frost to become edible; prior to cold weather, they are so astringent as to pucker the mouth.

At the southernmost point on this paddle trail, deep in the swamp forest, a three-way intersection is reached. Turn right to explore deeper into what is the Bosley Conservancy property. A series of fallen trees spans the narrow creek; several can be paddled over or

Persimmon tree

passed under, but eventually these strainers block further progress upstream. This is unfortunate for canoeists and kayakers, because at least a half mile of otherwise paddleable river lies upstream. However, there are sound ecological reasons to leave downed trees undisturbed. Their underwater branches provide shelter for fish and aquatic insects and slow the passage of floodwaters. Algae and bacteria grow on the limbs, forming the base of the food chain. This increased structural complexity, both aquatic and aerial, leads to a greater abundance and variety of species.

When you can go no farther upstream, return the way you came, and bear right at the three-way intersection. Within a few hundred yards, houses appear on the right bank, and any sense of being in a wild place disappears. However, the other side of the creek is marsh, and the scenery is still pleasant. Emerging from this narrow channel, you find yourself again at Eagle Cove. Paddle across it, round the corner, and see the marina a half mile ahead. This trip is roughly four miles of paddling, perhaps a bit more if you explore any of the several sloughs along the way. Be aware that during the autumn waterfowl hunting season, canoes and kayaks must stay well away from any occupied hunting blind. However, waterfowl hunting is prohibited on Sundays.

Directions

From Baltimore or Washington, DC, take I-95 north. Exit onto Route 24 south. Turn left onto Route 40. After passing the Otter Point Creek overlook (Smith Park), make the first right onto Otter Point Road. Follow it to the end.

Other Outdoor Recreational Opportunities Nearby

The Gunpowder Delta (described elsewhere in this book) is a similar freshwater marsh that is suitable for paddling. It is located about 10 miles southwest of Otter Point Creek.

RIVER OTTERS

It's a crisp, cold autumn dawn as I launch my canoe into the mirror-calm water. A chilly mist rises and swirls from the river, whose waters are still warmer than the air on this November day. I paddle around the point into a cove without houses or farms, and where few people venture. Ahead, a tree has fallen into the river, and its limbs and branches rise ghost-like from the mist. My mind on the day's plans, I fail to notice the objects on one large limb, until their movement catches my eye. Two river otters slide into the water without a sound.

I wish I had been paying more attention, because I've never before seen otters in the wild, and they are an uncommon sight on the tributaries of Chesapeake Bay. Once found in every state in the lower 48, river otters have been extirpated in much of the Midwest, and in arid regions where they were never common to start with. Without significant predators, otters have largely been reduced in number across North America by human activities, especially trapping. In Maryland, river otters may be trapped (but not hunted), in season with a permit, by Maryland residents only. Otters are rare enough in the two westernmost counties, Allegany and Garrett, that the skinned carcass must be presented to wildlife officers there.

Otters are mostly aquatic but can move around well on land. They occupy rivers, swamps, lakes, and tidal estuaries, wherever there are plenty of fish, their primary food. Since otters do not dig their own burrows, they coexist well with beavers, taking over bank tunnels and even beaver lodges for their own use. Females give birth in dry portions of these tunnels in a den lined with grass, leaves, and moss, usually in late winter. An average of two pups are born per litter, and are raised exclusively by the mother. Within two months of birth, pups enter the water; they are natural swimmers, and are soon finding fish to eat on their own. River otters typically live for about nine years in the wild, but may live for more than twice that in captivity.

Otters are well known for their playfulness, and for this reason they are favorites in zoos and aquariums. They often wrestle and chase each other, and enjoy sliding down muddy or snowy banks into water. My two otters live up to their reputation; a head pops up to my right, and I glimpse big brown eyes and long thick whiskers. This otter lets out an explosive snort, and then submarines back underwater; he is clearly upset to have me interrupt his morning on the river. I ship my paddle and float in silence, watching and waiting. For the next two or three minutes, the cove echoes with these snorts, as the two otters surface on all sides of me. All too soon, they are gone, but the magic of time spent in the company of wild creatures lingers long in my memory.

Virginia Canal

River Section: Virginia Canal circuit, using the Potomac River and C&O Canal
County: Loudon (Virginia)
Distance: About 3 miles
Difficulty: Moderate. Elementary whitewater
Hazards: Rocks, trees down in the river, high water
Highlights: An intimate side channel of the Potomac River
Nearby Canoe/Kayak Rental: None
Water Level Information: http://waterdata.usgs.gov/md/nwis
    /current?type=flow, scroll to Potomac River near Wash DC Little Falls
    (USGS 01646500); see text for details
More Information: C&O Canal National Historical Park, www.nps.gov
    /choh/index.htm, (301) 739-4200
Street Address: 13105 Violettes Lock Road, Darnestown, Maryland 20874
    (put-in parking lot)
GPS Coordinates: 39.067098, 77.328158 (Violettes Lock put-in parking lot)

Most of the rivers listed in this book are scenic flatwater, but here's one with elementary whitewater that can be managed by anyone who is able to maneuver a canoe or kayak accurately. It's a narrow, intimate side channel of the Potomac River west of Washington, with good scenery and wildlife. Best of all, the trip requires no shuttle; it's a circuit where you paddle back to your car.

The Virginia Canal, also known as the Patowmack Canal, is a part of a canal system older than the better-known C&O Canal. Built by a company that included George Washington as an investor, this canal permitted navigation around the rapids at Seneca. By about 1830, it had fallen into disrepair, and today it bears no resemblance at all to an artificial waterway.

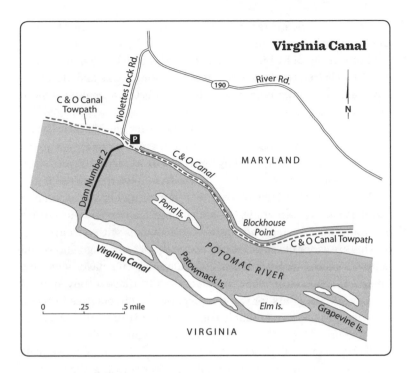

Virginia Canal

Trip Description

Begin (and end) your trip at the Violettes Lock parking area of the
C&O Canal National Historical Park. Neither drinking water nor
bathrooms is available here, so arrive with a full water bottle and an
empty bladder. Parking places are at a premium; arrive before 9 a.m.
or after 2 p.m. in warm weather. Carry your canoe or kayak across
the C&O Canal's Lock 23, then upstream on the towpath for 50 yards,
and finally down to the riverbank. The remains of Feeder Dam Number 2 back up the river here into a long slackwater known as Seneca
Lake, popular with powerboaters and water-skiers. Paddle across
the wide Potomac well above the rubble of Dam Number 2. On the far
Virginia shore, look for an opening in the trees that is located about
100 feet above the rapids formed by the crumbling dam.

Entry into this intimate stream opens up a whole different world.
Tall trees arch gracefully overhead; the canal is shady and cool on
even the hottest summer days. There is a continuous current here,
even at low water, so paddle only to steer, relax in available eddies to

enjoy the scenery, and take your time. Stay alert for downed trees in the water and avoid them even before you think you need to. Because the Potomac is such a big river, it carries a lot of debris when in flood. That debris frequently gets tangled up among rocks and along the riverbanks in a chute as narrow as the Virginia Canal, making it more hazardous than would be typical.

Keep an eye peeled for wildlife as you paddle the Virginia Canal. Turtles and herons (both great blue and green-backed) frequent these backwaters, although they tend to be a bit skittish. You're more likely to hear the plop of a turtle diving from a log than to see it and to glimpse the wrong end of a heron as it flaps off downriver than to watch it feeding peacefully. On hot summer days, water snakes are common. These thick, chocolate-brown snakes with obscure patterning are generally harmless, although they can be pugnacious and deliver a sharp bite if provoked. They also give off a nasty-smelling, mucouslike secretion when handled. Finally, these woody sloughs are favorite hangouts for wood ducks. Nesting in cavities in trees, male wood ducks are probably the most beautiful of all our ducks. Count yourself lucky if you see one of these avian jewels.

Several small rapids and riffles punctuate the canal. Local paddling clubs find the Virginia Canal a perfect training site for novices enjoying their first taste of whitewater, and informal classes are frequently encountered. The current flow is fast enough to create visible eddy lines, but not so violent as to flip over the unwary canoeist or kayaker. All the rapids are open down the middle but require some elementary steering skills. A pool for recovery and relaxation follows each.

The Virginia Canal is divided into three visually distinct segments. The first 200 yards runs straight and fairly narrow, with a steep bank on the right side. The final rapid of this section drops about one foot over a ledge where experienced kayakers gather to work and play in the whitewater. A large, deep pool follows, marking the start of the second segment of river. Here the water splits among a maze of channels, separated by rock outcrops and small islands. Selecting a route with enough water can be a problem through here at dead low-water levels, and a judicious reading of current flow is helpful. The end of this second section is marked by a channel on river left that flows back into the main Potomac around the west end of Elm Island. Continue downstream, however, into the third segment of the canal. Here the river widens, flowing over a shallow bed of stones and gravel unobstructed by rapids or rock outcroppings. If the water is clear, note the many tiny shells of freshwater clams and mussels that litter the bottom; this shallow, cool, sheltered environment with a steady flow of oxygenated water is a nearly perfect habitat for these poorly appreciated animals.

After another third of a mile, the Virginia Canal merges with the main Potomac. Turn left, around the end of Elm Island, and paddle upstream against the current. The goal is to cross the Potomac to its Maryland shore; to do so, you must traverse the upstream end of Grapevine Island, which here divides the main Potomac for more than a mile. Once you've attained the head of the island, aim for the gap in the trees that marks a pipeline crossing. Do not, however, take out here for the portage to the C&O Canal, because the canal has diverged from the river at this point. Instead, continue upstream 100 yards to a well-used beach for a flat, 30-yard carry.

Once on the re-watered canal, proceed upstream (left). A remarkable number of paw paw trees line the canal here. In late August, many bear edible fruits that resemble green, fat, stubby bananas. Scoop out the custardlike fruit inside for an enjoyable snack. There are also a few persimmon trees overhanging the water. The fruit, an orangish sphere about the size of a golf ball, requires cold weather to become palatable. Ripe specimens will have a brownish tinge and will virtually fall into your hand when cradled gently. Eating an unripe persimmon, however, is one of life's most unpleasant gustatory experiences, for it resembles nothing so much as a mouthful of raw cotton.

This entire circuit is just a bit over three miles long. If you take your time, loaf, practice eddy turns, and work on your tan, it can be a satisfying half-day trip. Couple it with some good friends and a picnic lunch and you have a recipe for a great day on the river.

A final note of caution: the Potomac is a powerful river at moderate to high water levels, and at those times it is no place for anyone except experienced whitewater kayakers. To find out about water levels before you leave home, go to the US Geological Survey website, http://waterdata.usgs.gov/md/nwis/current?type=flow and look for the Little Falls gauge reading (USGS 01646500). Expect to do some scraping if the gauge reading is below 2.8 feet. Between 2.8 and 3.5 feet is ideal. If it is between 3.5 and 4.0 feet you should not venture out unless you have significant whitewater experience; above 4.0 feet, you would be wise to curl up at home with a good book.

Note: Access to the Virginia Canal may be limited during the presidency of Donald Trump as a security precaution since he owns a golf course nearby and sometimes plays there or hosts other dignitaries.

Directions

From the Capital Beltway (I-495), take Route 190 (River Road) west. Proceed 11.3 miles, through the village of Potomac, and turn left onto Violettes Lock Road. Follow the road to its end at the parking area.

Other Outdoor Recreational Opportunities Nearby

The C&O canal towpath is 184 miles in length and is excellent for cycling, walking, birding, botanizing, and backpacking.

MUSSELS

Freshwater mussels may be one of the least-known and most poorly appreciated groups of animals found in Maryland. These shelled animals are molluscs, a taxonomic group that also includes snails, clams, and oysters. They have two shells (and so are called bivalves), a heavy, wedge-shaped foot that they use to move and anchor themselves, and a pair of extendable siphons. Freshwater mussels typically sit half-buried in river-bottom gravel with their shells partly open, filtering the passing flow of water for food.

Because they are immobile and feed by filtration, mussels are exquisitely sensitive to water quality. Pollutants in the water column tend to accumulate in mussel tissues; in fact, analysis of tissue has been used to identify an upstream pollution source via its unique chemical signature. Massive mussel die-offs have been documented in response to major pollution events upstream. Unable to move, mussels are tireless monitors of water quality.

In addition to being affected by chemical pollution, mussels are sensitive to sedimentation. Changes in upstream land use, such as deforestation and development, usually cause erosion. Increased loads of silt and mud eventually fill the interstices in bottom gravels that mussels require and make feeding and breathing more difficult.

Construction of dams has also affected mussel populations and their diversity. Mussels require sun-warmed waters to reproduce; many dams release water from the cold bottom of the reservoir. Although this release is often a boon to trout, it means that mussels may continue to exist for years but never reproduce.

In optimum habitat, fertilization results in a free-living larval stage called a glochidium. This tiny, clamlike organism settles to the river bottom and awaits a passing fish. When a fish brushes the open shells of the glochidium, the valves close around a gill or fin. The little mussel obtains nourishment from the fish for a period of time and then eventually drops off. If the glochidium fails to attach to a fish, or falls off in unsuitable habitat, it dies. Some scientists believe that declines in mussel numbers and distribution may be due in part to the decline in anadromous fish populations that serve as glochidium hosts.

North America is home to the greatest diversity of freshwater mussels in the world. Unfortunately, 43 percent of its 300 species are extinct, endangered, or threatened. Unobtrusive and sensitive, freshwater mussels act as canaries in the environmental coal mines, and their continued existence is largely in our hands.

Upper Gunpowder River

River Section: Section 1: Masemore Road to Monkton Road
   Section 2: Monkton Road to Sparks Road
County: Baltimore
Distance: Section 1: 7.8 miles
   Section 2: 5.3 miles
Difficulty: Moderate. Flat flowing water, elementary whitewater
Hazards: Possible trees down in the river, rocks
Highlights: A lovely, narrow river with clear, clean, cold water flowing through
   a shallow wooded gorge entirely within Gunpowder Falls State Park
Water Level Information: https://waterdata.usgs.gov/md/nwis
   /current?type=flow, scroll to Gunpowder Falls near Parkton
   (USGS 01581920); see text for details
Nearby Canoe/Kayak Rental: None
More Information: Gunpowder Falls State Park, http://dnr.maryland.gov
   /publiclands/pages/central/gunpowder.aspx, (410) 592-2897
Street Address: Section 1: put-in near 17700 Masemore Road; take-out near
   1810 Monkton Road
   Section 2: put-in near 1810 Monkton Road; take-out near 1207 Sparks Road
GPS Coordinates: 39.611359, 76.682775 (Masemore Road); 39.578617,
   76.618054 (Monkton Road); 39.539695, 76.639211 (Sparks Road)

The Gunpowder river gathers its waters from the rich, rolling
countryside of north central Maryland and southern Pennsylvania. Rather sparsely populated, with only small, quaint hamlets, the land is dissected by a number of tiny streams, many of which contain viable populations of native brook trout. Yet almost as soon as these rivulets coalesce into something of size, the Gunpowder's waters are dammed into Prettyboy Reservoir. Between the outflow of Prettyboy Dam and the backwaters behind Loch Raven Dam lies

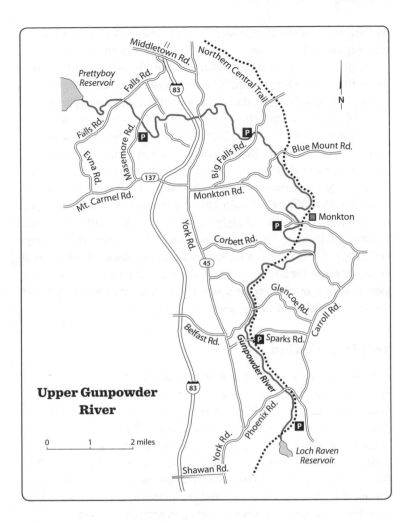

Upper Gunpowder River

0   1   2 miles

a beautiful wooded valley that is one of the Baltimore metropolitan area's finest recreational resources.

Known among paddlers as the Upper Gunpowder, the river flows cool and clear year-round. Even in the driest weather, there's a minimal flow of water in the river to maintain the fish and aquatic insect populations. In summer, the coolest spot around can be found in the steep, wooded gorge just below Prettyboy Dam. The water coming out of the bottom of the reservoir is in the 40° to 50° range, air-conditioning the river valley. The narrowness of the river (it is never more than about 50 feet wide) and the shade of the overhanging mature trees of the Gunpowder Falls State Park ensure that the water does not heat up appreciably during its flow to Loch Raven.

Appropriate water levels are important for a fun paddling trip down the Upper Gunpowder. You'll want to check the latest conditions at the US Geological Service website, http://waterdata.usgs .gov/md/nwis/current?type=flow. Scroll down to "Gunpowder Falls near Parkton, MD" (USGS 01581920) for the upper section (Masemore Road to Monkton Road); you should have a minimum of 2.00 feet for a trip with little scraping. For the lower section, Monkton Road to Sparks, scroll down to "Gunpowder Falls at Glencoe, MD" (USGS 01582500); you should have a minimum flow of 2.2 feet on this gauge. Perhaps surprisingly, the river often has sufficient water in times of drought. This is because water is released from Prettyboy Dam to fill up Loch Raven Reservoir downstream—the source of drinking water for Baltimore. Consider more than 3.00 feet on these gauges to be a maximum for a safe trip unless you have significant experience with whitewater paddling.

Trip Description

Section 1: Masemore Road to Monkton Road

With sufficient water, begin your trip at Masemore Road. This is the uppermost easily accessible road crossing, and this upper part of the river is the most pleasantly intimate section. There's room to park about a dozen cars here, with good access to the river but no facilities. Initially, the river flows over shallow gravel bars, with a few riffles thrown in for variety. Vegetation overhangs the riverbanks, so keep to the middle. The flow is constant and fast in this upper section, and the first few miles can be covered quickly and with little effort.

Scenery along the Gunpowder is beautiful. Gunpowder Falls State Park runs along both banks of the river, preserving it from development. Rock outcrops decorated with ferns are common, and hillsides full of large trees stretch up from the river. In some places, rich floodplains on the insides of bends present a riot of vegetation. Spring wildflowers are superb.

On narrow, fast-flowing streams like this, paddlers must use caution to avoid trees that have fallen into the river. Known as strainers because they hang up solid objects like canoes, kayaks, and their human paddlers while allowing water to pass through, these hazards can be deadly on flooded creeks. At normal water levels on the Gunpowder, strainers can still result in a flip, a swim, and a broached boat. Stay well away from downed trees, aggressively paddling your canoe or kayak out of the way well before you think you have to. Even on a river as benign as the Upper Gunpowder, strainers deserve a healthy dose of respect.

Rapids appear at only two locations. About a half mile downriver of York Road (Maryland Route 45), an old rock dam spans the river at a hard right turn. There is an opening near the right shore. The water drops about a foot into a fast, straight chute filled with small waves. The other rapid, about a hundred yards of moderate rapids, is found just below Big Falls Road. Here, the river has been constricted by fill from the adjacent quarry, and rock rubble fills the channel. At higher water levels, this rapid will give a bouncy but straightforward ride.

Below the Big Falls Road quarry, the Gunpowder resumes its serene flow through forested parkland. A recommended take-out is at the Monkton Road bridge. Wheelchair-accessible bathrooms, water, picnic tables, trash cans, and information are available at Monkton station, just 100 yards uphill from the river. The distance from Masemore Road to Monkton Road is 7.8 miles.

Section 2: Monkton Road to Sparks Road

In summertime low water, the section from Monkton Road downstream to Sparks Road is recommended. This route avoids the shallow rapids at the quarry described previously, and the river's flow is augmented by input from Little Falls. Although slightly wider and slower moving, the Gunpowder is still beautiful, shady, and cool. During these times, you'll scrape your kayak or canoe over gravel bars and riffles that mark the downstream ends of long, deep pools. In a few places, you may even have to get out and walk, dragging your boat behind you. But on a hot summer day, a fluvial walk is refreshing. In fact, this is a great place to tow an old truck inner tube or two full of kids. Most people who tube the Upper Gunpowder do so only once; the chill waters linger in memory even after bones and muscles rewarm. But with a canoe or kayak to haul snacks and beverages and to provide a place to warm up, such a trip is memorable for its carefree enjoyment.

By summer, the river banks are a riot of lush vegetation, with jewelweed, coneflower, Joe-Pye weed, boneset, and New York ironweed flourishing in the rich, moist, alluvial soil. Bees, wasps, and bugs of all sorts congregate on the flowerheads in search of nectar and plant juices. The structural complexity of this herbaceous layer provides prime habitat for web-spinning spiders; the morning dew glints jewel-like from their tracery. Bird life along the river corridor is plentiful, with the young of the year now grown to adolescence. With food plentiful, living is easy, but the shortening days already portend the coming of cold weather, and animals use this time to store winter reserves.

After just a bit more than five miles of paddling, this trip's end is signaled by the white bridge that carries Sparks Road over the river. Haul your boat from the water a few yards below the bridge on the left side (as you face downriver). There is a parking lot for perhaps a dozen cars within 50 yards, with more parking on the far side of the Northern Central Railroad Trail. If you have only one vehicle, or do not want to bother setting a car shuttle, it is possible to use the Northern Central Railroad Trail to bicycle (or even walk) back to your car. The trail parallels the Gunpowder as far north as Monkton.

Directions

From the Baltimore Beltway (I-695), take I-83 north. To reach the Masemore Road put-in, exit the interstate at Mt. Carmel Road (Route 137). Turn left (west). The first right turn is Masemore Road; follow it to the river. To reach Monkton, return to Mt. Carmel Road. Cross over I-83. The road ends at York Road (Route 45). Turn right, go 100 yards, and turn left on Monkton Road. Follow it to the river. Access to the river is on the concrete right-of-way at the southeastern corner of the bridge. Obey the nearby No Parking signs; parking is available about 50 yards up the hill on a spur road. Sparks Road is also easily accessed from York Road, Route 45. Take York Road south from Monkton for 3 miles and turn left on Sparks Road. Follow it to the river.

Other Outdoor Recreational Opportunities Nearby

There are many fine hiking trails in Gunpowder Falls State Park, which occupies both sides of the river for most of the described river runs.

RIVER FLOODPLAINS AND
AMPHIBIAN BREEDING SITES

Floodplains like those along Maryland's Piedmont rivers provide a unique habitat for certain kinds of plants and animals. Each spring, heavy rains bring the river out of its banks, and silt-laden water spreads out over the floodplain. These irregular but consistent events provide plants growing in the floodplain with a fresh pulse of nutrient-rich alluvial soil, decaying vegetation, seeds, and moisture. Thus the floodplain receives the natural equivalent of a good fertilizing. Of course, a major flood also has a down side: it will scour low-lying areas of vegetation, weaken the root systems of large trees, and generally subject the flora to erosional stress and localized extinctions.

Seasonal flooding also creates temporary ponds in low-lying areas of the floodplain just beyond the primary banks of the river. These vernal pools usually dry up by midsummer, but over their short lifetimes they provide important habitat for the living organisms of a river valley. Perhaps the most significant role of these ephemeral wetlands is as a breeding ground for several species of amphibians. The vernal ponds along the upper Gunpowder River are among the best local examples.

The first warm, rainy night of late winter or early spring signals the start of the breeding season for many frogs and salamanders. Leaving estivation sites deep in the earth on surrounding hillsides, adult animals migrate toward the floodplain, drawn by some primitive, unknowable urge. Wood frogs are the earliest-breeding species in Maryland. They can sometimes be found in these vernal ponds even when a skim of ice extends outward from the edges, as early as February. A dark mask or line extending horizontally across the face from ear to ear identifies the wood frog. Sound is the best way to locate breeding frogs; each species has its own characteristic call. The wood frog makes a raspy sound, halfway between a quack and a cluck. Its breeding season is short, ranging from a few days to a few weeks, depending on weather conditions. After eggs are laid in the vernal ponds, adults disperse back into the surrounding

(continued)

forests, leaving the developing young at the mercy of predators and harsh weather.

Breeding almost as early as the wood frog is the spring peeper. It is perhaps the most common of our frogs and is familiar to almost everyone. Its long breeding season and noisy call make it synonymous with the coming of spring. Identified by an X-shaped design on its back, the frog is tiny (with a body less than two inches long) and amazingly hard to find even when it is vocalizing. Its distinctive call is a short, sharp note or peep. Males stake out a territory at the edge of a vernal pond and sing to advertise their readiness to mate.

Still later in the season, after wood frogs have left but while peepers are still active, American toads join the chorus. Their call is a loud trill of closely spaced notes. Once again, males stake out a territory, and they will clasp (or attempt to clasp) almost anything that moves past—a female, another male, or even an otherwise inanimate object. For this reason, males have a second call in their repertoire, a "get-off-my-back" call. If you stay long enough at an active breeding site, you should be able to distinguish this different call.

These breeding amphibians are sometimes active all day at the short peak of their breeding season, but activity really picks up after dark. For this reason, early evening is the best time to visit and observe this fascinating rite of spring. Armed with hip waders and a good flashlight, make your way to the edge of a vernal pond and wait until the animals get acclimated to your presence. You can then use your flashlight to spotlight singing amphibians, find mating pairs, or locate egg masses. Fortunately, most frogs and toads seem to remain oblivious to this intrusion on their sex lives. Since the sounds of breeding frogs are among the earliest signs of spring, a visit to one of these vernal ponds is a great way to reconnect with the natural world after a long winter inside.

Monocacy River

River Section: Buckeystown Community Park to Mouth of Monocacy
boat ramp
Counties: Frederick, Montgomery
Distance: 9.5 miles
Difficulty: Easy. Flowing flatwater, elementary whitewater
Hazards: High water
Water Level Information: https://waterdata.usgs.gov/md/nwis
/current?type=flow, scroll to the Potomac River Basin, Monocacy River
at Frederick gauge (USGS 01642190); see text for details
Highlights: An enjoyable paddle on lazy river flowing past farms, fields,
and riparian forests, concluding with views of a historic aqueduct
Nearby Canoe/Kayak Rental: None
More Information: Frederick County Parks and Recreation, http://recreater
.com/204/Buckeystown-Park, (301) 600-1646; C&O Canal National
Historical Park, www.nps.gov/choh/index.htm, (301) 739-4200
Street Address: 7221 Michaels Mill Road, Buckeystown, Maryland 21717;
none (Mouth of Monocacy boat ramp)
GPS Coordinates: 39.327968, 77.415880 (Buckeystown Community Park);
39.224514, 77.450030 (Mouth of Monocacy boat ramp)

The Monocacy may be the quintessential Maryland river; neither tidal nor montane, it runs through the rich heartland of well-kept farms and low rolling pasturage. The Monocacy seems moderate in all its aspects: of medium volume with only a slight gradient; with little stream-side development but not wild either; having few major environmental problems but accumulating a variety of minor insults. A paddling trip down the Monocacy will never be the most scenic, the most exciting, or the most pristine, but the river will impress you, much like an old friend, with its quiet good nature. There is much to appreciate in the Monocacy, and for that reason it has been declared an official Scenic River by the state of Maryland.

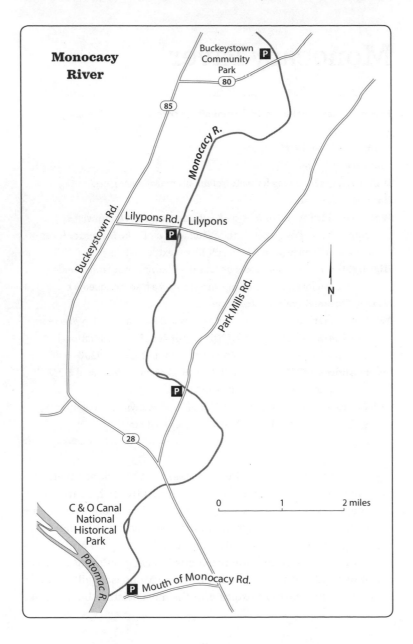

The Monocacy drains several counties in south-central Pennsylvania, as well as parts of Frederick, Carroll, and Montgomery Counties in Maryland. From the time its waters enter the state near Emmitsburg, it flows slowly for 57 miles in meandering bends southward toward the Potomac. Fine agricultural fields line most of the river, although a border of riparian habitat in the form of big old trees invariably buffers the river corridor and gives a sense of isolation to the paddler. Very little of the riverbank is publicly owned, but access is good at a variety of road crossings. When water levels are moderate, you can choose whatever section of river appeals to you, making judicious use of a good map. In summer, however, low water limits your paddling possibilities to the lowermost portion of the Monocacy. The trip outlined here runs from Buckeystown Community Park to the mouth near Dickerson; these 9.5 miles almost always have enough water to float your canoe or kayak, although in late summer and fall you may have to get out and haul your boat over a few rocks or gravel bars. The Monocacy River at Frederick gauge (see the key above for the web address) should read between 1.7 and about 4.0 feet.

Trip Description

Begin your voyage on the Monocacy at Buckeystown Community Park, where there is a portable toilet, a playground, a picnic shelter, and ample parking. Carry your boat to the far end of the parking lot and along a short path to where a set of concrete steps leads down the steep bank to river level. Here, in the deep shade of large bankside trees, the river dances as it flows fast over a gravelly bed. Soon, however, the pace slows as the Monocacy settles down to its typical speed. The river is about fifty yards in width, with near-vertical banks about a dozen feet high on both sides. The riverbed is mostly flat for its entire width, meaning that at summer low water the Monocacy is wide but very shallow. Centuries of erosion off the surrounding uplands have brought sand and gravel to the river; freshwater clams abound in these small cobbles. Filamentous algae might be expected in a shallow, slow-flowing river, but they are uncommon, probably because frequent high water events prevent attachment and growth. Draining a large and mostly agricultural watershed, the Monocacy fills and even overflows its banks on a surprisingly frequent basis, anytime there is a heavy rain.

In its initial mile, the Monocacy inscribes a broad curve through the landscape. Large trees line the bank, mostly silver maple and sycamore. From May until mid-August, these arboreal giants host Baltimore orioles, the Maryland state bird. These orange and black songsters construct pendulous nests high in these trees, and often flit across the river. The best way to see orioles is to familiarize yourself with their song before the trip, then scan the treetops when you hear it. Binoculars will be helpful with getting a close look at these birds, who rarely come down to river level. Other birds commonly seen along the Monocacy are kingfishers, great blue herons, and wood ducks. Less frequently seen but still present are pileated woodpeckers, warblers (in late spring), osprey, and even the occasional bald eagle.

The Monocacy then runs fairly straight in a southward direction for several miles. After passing under the first bridge (Lilypons Road), stay right to avoid a shallow gravel bar. Just before reaching the second bridge (Park Mills Road, about halfway through the trip), the river runs over three small rapids, one after another. At low water, these can hang up your boat, especially if it is made of aluminum. However, the rapids are not dangerous (unless the river is very high), and they may provide some spice to your trip at more moderate water levels. For a shorter trip, you can access the river here at Park Mills Road (there is a fisherman's parking lot), either taking out after 5.8 miles or starting here for a 3.6-mile run down to Mouth of Monocacy.

The Monocacy is admirably adapted to a summer canoe or kayak trip with kids because it's a great river for wading, dabbling, and just generally messing around in water. Choose a gravel bar on which to pull out your canoe, and get wet. The river's depth averages only a foot or two, even near the center; there is no well-defined channel. The flow is continuous but never fast, and even small children are not overwhelmed by the current. The bed—of cobbles, sand, and gravel—gives a fairly good footing, although everyone should wear old sneakers or water shoes and use care when wading. Bring along a surf mat or old truck inner tube for the kids to float in; adults can even position a low-slung beach chair in a foot or so of flowing water, sitting in water-cooled comfort while the children romp. You might even try "rapid sitting." This oxymoronic activity involves finding a small rapid or riffle, positioning yourself on a flat river-bottom rock, and trying to avoid being swept downstream by the current. If you park yourself in the lee of a larger rock, the turbulence formed by the aerated water gives the feeling of being in a jacuzzi. When the temperature hits 90° and you're tired of sitting at home in the air conditioning, this is the only way to beat the heat outdoors.

While you're sitting in the river, pull up a rock from the riverbed wherever there's a good current. In the Monocacy, you'll find it loaded with snails and aquatic insects. Most common are caddis flies, insects that are wormlike in shape but possess legs, with which they squirm over the rocks. Caddis flies cement together tiny stones to form rude huts, which help to protect them from predators; a square foot of rock surface may have dozens of these curious structures. Caddis flies spin a web of fibers that they set out in the current much like nets, capturing whatever drifts downstream and happens to get caught. Although caddis fly larvae are the most common aquatic insects on the Monocacy, you may also find a few water pennies and mayflies. Together, the number and diversity of these insects are an index to the water quality of any flowing river or stream, and they are used by scientists for that purpose.

What does the aquatic insect index say about the water quality of the Monocacy? It's a mixed verdict: somewhat degraded, but not extremely so—about what you might expect of a creek running through mostly agricultural land. The input of nutrients from animal feces enriches the water and encourages the growth of algae on rocks. Fencing in pastures could go a long way toward curing this problem. At certain times of the year, pesticides and herbicides can get into the river, especially after heavy rains or during the spring thaw. Overall, however, the Monocacy is in pretty good shape, and its water quality will not negatively affect your trip.

Another two miles of paddling will bring you to the third road bridge (Route 28) of this trip. A shallow ledge of rocks spans the river almost under the bridge, making a pleasant riffle at higher water and a possible drag at low water levels. In another mile, the river seems to disappear, as an island occupies the middle. There are routes through on the right and in the center, but the passage on the left is more pleasant, featuring a quick, deep current. Protected by a gravel bar, this left chute is not visible until you're almost on top of it.

Signs of civilization now mark the end of the trip. The river passes under a sizzling high-tension line, carrying electricity from the nearby Dickerson generating plant. The ruins of an old bridge piling appear at a turn, and just past this the C&O Canal aqueduct and Potomac River emerge from the haze. Take out at the National Park Service boat ramp and parking lot on the left; there are trash cans and a vault toilet here.

The Monocacy aqueduct is a marvel of nineteenth-century engineering. Spanning the Monocacy River, it carries the C&O Canal for 516 feet on seven arches, tall enough to withstand the largest floods. The aqueduct is constructed of a beautiful granite quarried at the nearby Sugarloaf Mountain.

Finally, the Monocacy is a fine fishing river. Sunnies and smallmouth abound, and they are usually easy to catch. Angling seems about equally divided between bank fishing, wading, and casting from a canoe or small boat, so take your pick. Once again, it's not the best fishing in the state, but it can be fun, especially for novices.

Directions

From Baltimore, take I-70 west to Frederick. Exit at Route 85 south toward Buckeystown. Go 9 miles, then turn left onto Route 80, Fingerboard Road. Continue for 2 miles, turning left on Michael Mills Road at the sign for Buckeystown Community Park.

From Washington, DC, take I-270 northwest toward Frederick. Take exit 26, Urbanna, getting on Route 80 west. Continue on Route 80 for 4 miles. Immediately after crossing the Monocacy River, turn right on Michael Mills Road and enter the Buckeystown Community Park.

To reach the take-out from the put-in, turn left out of the Buckeystown Community Park, then right on Fingerboard Road, Route 80. Go 2 miles, then turn left on Route 85. At a fork in the road, bear left; Route 85 turns into Route 28. Cross the Monocacy River and continue south. Turn right onto Mouth of Monocacy Road and follow it to the end, parking in the boat launch lot.

Other Outdoor Recreational Opportunities Nearby

Birders and gardeners will not want to miss Lilypons Water Gardens, located on Lilypons Road just east of the river. The gardens are situated on a broad floodplain, and the owners raise and sell all sorts of plants, although they specialize in aquatic plants. The water lilies bloom in July. The wetland habitats attract a variety of water birds; birders should bring a spotting scope. Sugarloaf Mountain, just a few miles away, is a pleasant site for hiking. The C&O Canal towpath, within yards of the take-out, has 184.5 miles of hiking available.

RIPARIAN HABITAT

Of all the different kinds of habitat found across the face of Maryland, perhaps none is as rich with living organisms as riparian habitat. Defined as the land edge of streams, rivers, lakes, and other bodies of water, riparian habitat is almost invariably a wetland, with hydric soils and characteristic plant species. Yet most of us do not consider the miles and miles of Maryland forested riparian habitat bordering our flowing rivers and creeks to be wetland. For this reason, the economic and ecological value of such riparian habitat is only poorly appreciated.

Forested riparian habitat has a great many environmental benefits. Streamside buffers of trees act as filters, removing excess nutrients from groundwater, decomposing pollutants, and removing bacteria. The roots of trees stabilize streambanks and prevent erosion, while the boles and forest floor detritus slow the speed of floodwaters, causing the deposition of sediment. These same trees shade the creek, creating a cooler, more humid microclimate important to organisms in the water as well as those on the land. Indeed, forested riparian zones are incredibly rich in animal life. Amphibians, so dependent on water for much of their life cycles, are obligately associated species. Among the mammals, otter, beaver, and mink are the most common riparian inhabitants. Bird life is especially rich in riparian zones; studies invariably show a higher density of breeding birds there than in nearby upland sites. Migrating forest species, probably using rivers to navigate, stop over here as well. The role of riparian habitat as corridors for wildlife movements between larger reserves has only recently become appreciated.

(continued)

Historically, about 70 percent of North America's riparian habitat has been lost to forest clearance, drainage for agriculture, and development. Much of what is left, fortunately, will probably remain preserved, since its importance is now recognized. Although some towns in Maryland are built on river floodplains, more often local and state governments have purchased such lands and converted them into parks. Indeed, many of the trips described in this book traverse riparian zones. Ultimately, the highest and best use of forested riparian habitat may be for the enjoyment and edification of us humans; if it is only by coincidence that such a use is also the most beneficial for wildlife, then so be it.

Antietam Creek

River Section: Route 68 to the Potomac River
County: Washington
Distance: 13.3 miles; shorter trips possible
Difficulty: Moderate. Flowing water with many riffles and small Class I
    rapids; one Class II rapid
Hazards: Trees down in the river (strainers), especially at bridge piers
Water Level Information: https://waterdata.usgs.gov/md/nwis
    /current?type=flow, scroll down to the Potomac River Basin, Antietam
    Creek near Sharpsburg, MD, gauge (USGS 01619500); see text for details
Highlights: A beautiful Piedmont river whose banks are lined with spring
    wildflowers and which passes through a historic battlefield
Nearby Canoe/Kayak Rental: Antietam Creek Canoe, (240) 447-0444,
    www.acckap.com
More Information: Antietam Creek Canoe, (240) 447-0444, www.acckap
    .com; American Whitewater, www.americanwhitewater.com
Street Address: 18934 Lappans Road, Boonsboro, Maryland 21713
    (Devil's Backbone Park); near 17850 Canal Road, Sharpsburg, Maryland
    21782 (C&O Canal towpath)
GPS Coordinates: 39.538472, 77.710171 (Devil's Backbone Park launch
    point); 39.419040, 77.745748 (C&O Canal towpath take-out)

Antietam Creek flows quietly over rocks and riffles, meandering
across a pastoral landscape, shaded by tall sycamores and silver maples. It's one of Maryland's most beautiful streams. But most
Americans know the Antietam place name for an altogether different reason: here, in 1862, two armies clashed in a battle that still
holds the dubious distinction of being the bloodiest day in American history. More than 23,000 men from the Union and Confederate
armies were killed or wounded near the banks of Antietam Creek

on September 17 of that year. The fighting was savage, the blood-shed horrific, and the bravery unsurpassed. The consequence of this battle was central to American history; the Union strategic victory permitted Abraham Lincoln to issue the Emancipation Proclamation, freeing the slaves in rebellious states and changing the purpose of the war from the political (state's rights) to the moral (eradication of slavery). It is not an overstatement to say that Antietam was and still is the most significant place and event in Maryland history.

Despite its fame and importance, Antietam remains the best preserved of all the Civil War battlefields, appearing much as it did more than 150 years ago. There is virtually no tourism industry in the adjacent town of Sharpsburg, and the landscape is still almost exclusively agricultural. Antietam is a place that invites contemplation, reflection, and introspection.

What makes this paddling trip unique is that one of the three major portions of the battle took place along the banks of Antietam Creek, so you get to paddle though that hallowed ground, a place where thousands of Americans fought and hundreds died. It's hard to avoid imagining what it must have been like on that late summer's day, along the banks of this very creek, as you pass under Burnside Bridge.

Trip Description

Begin your paddling trip from Devil's Backbone Park, owned by Washington County, where Route 68 crosses Antietam Creek. There are restrooms and water, but the parking area is rather small, so come early if you've chosen a holiday weekend. Put in on the water just below the dam. Should you need to rent one or more canoes or kayaks (reservations required), or if you only want more information, contact Antietam Creek Canoe, located just across the road from the park.

Antietam Creek is a flowing river, so you'll have to set a shuttle before launching your boat, and you'll need a second car. After unloading, leave at least one trip participant with the gear, and the two (or more) drivers should proceed to the take-out. Leave one car there, and use the second car to drive back to Devil's Backbone Park. Make sure all drivers go down the river with their car keys, safely secured in a waterproof bag that is in turn secured to the boat. At

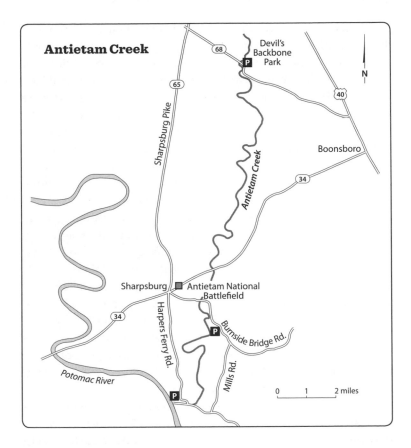

trip's end, just reverse this process. Finding the most efficient way to run a car shuttle is one of paddling's higher order skills; it takes lots of practice.

You have two choices for a take-out location: where Antietam Creek runs into the Potomac River (13.3 miles from Devil's Backbone) or near Burnside Bridge, where Burnside Bridge Road runs alongside the creek (about 10 miles). Parking is limited to a half dozen spaces at the latter take-out, while there is plenty of parking along the Potomac River. While there are three other locations where public roads cross Antietam Creek, all of the very limited parking there is on private property.

Once on the river, the woes of shuttling fall behind and the magic of river travel in a small boat takes over. Antietam Creek flows along at a good pace, and riffles and small rapids punctuate the run. Try to avoid rocks; aim for the open chute between them. And keep paddling! Having a paddle in the water helps maintain stability. Should you become stuck on a rock, lean into the rock and try to slide your boat off it. Of greater concern than rocks are strainers: trees that have fallen into the river, blocking part or even all of the creek. If there is not an obvious way around such a strainer, land your boat on the bank, get out, and scout the best route. If none is possible, portage. Of special concern are piles of strainers that sometime accumulate on bridge piers; use extra caution where bridges cross the river.

Despite these cautions, strainers are rarely a problem on Antietam Creek. Focus on enjoying your river experience. The water is almost always clear on the Antietam, because of the unique geology of the watershed. This area of Washington County is underlain by limestone, a rock that forms cracks and fissures over time. Water percolates into these gaps and down into the water table, eventually re-emerging as springs. For this reason, the water is often clearer than on nearby creeks. In addition, the flow is less variable after rainstorms. The river level doesn't rise significantly unless a lot of rain falls; conversely, the creek holds its water in times of drought. Nevertheless, it's worthwhile to check the gauge before leaving home. See the key above for the web address; the Antietam Creek at Sharpsburg gauge should read between 2.5 and 5.0 feet.

The banks of Antietam Creek are well known for their displays of spring wildflowers. The diversity of blooms is, in turn, caused by the soils descended from limestone. Farmers call such soil "sweet"; they mean it has a basic pH that permits plants to get minerals from the soil with greater ease. In late April, the banks of the Antietam are lined with superb displays of Virginia bluebells, whose sky-blue flowers form pendulous clusters. Rock faces often sport wild columbines, uncommon elsewhere in Maryland. Other spring wildflowers to look for include spring beauties, wild ginger, toothwort, bloodroot, violets, trout lilies, and Dutchman's breeches (to name a few). It's a true garden of delights that you paddle past.

Use the road bridges to gauge your progress. The first, Manor Church Road, is at about mile 2 from Devil's Backbone Park. The second, Keedysville Road, is a further three miles. In another mile and a half, the right bank becomes public property, part of the Antietam National Battlefield. Route 34 crosses the Antietam at about mile 8, and Burnside Bridge Road at mile 9. Just beyond this point, the iconic Burnside Bridge appears. Named for the inept Union commander of this part of the battlefield, Ambrose Burnside (whose prodigious whiskers gave us the moniker "side burns"), the bridge is one of the most famous landmarks in American history. And you get to paddle under it, seeing and experiencing it from a perspective few others do.

The battle around Burnside Bridge took place just after noon on September 17, 1862. Only 400 Confederate sharpshooters occupied the steep hill on river right, protected by trenches and boulders. Burnside had 12,000 men, but sent them at the bridge piecemeal. For reasons unknown, the men were ordered to cross the bridge instead of just wading Antietam Creek. It took several hours for the Union troops to accomplish a crossing, at great cost, long enough for the rest of the Confederate army to arrive on the field.

Just 100 yards past Burnside Bridge, Antietam Creek drops over a two-foot high ledge, a rapid known as Molly's Hole. It was actually constructed in part by the US Geological Survey so that they could install a gauge to measure river flow. Paddlers use this, the Sharpsburg gauge, to estimate whether the water level in Antietam Creek is appropriate for canoeing, kayaking, and tubing (see water level information at the beginning of this chapter).

Another several miles of pleasant cruising lies ahead, the river punctuated by small riffles and flowing past field and forest. Finally, just after a bend, the sound of whitewater fills the narrow valley, and a rapid with whitewater and small waves appears. At higher water levels, get out of your boat and scout this fairly long (50 yards) Class II rapid. Make sure there are no strainers in either the river or against the bridge piers at rapid's end. It's not a difficult rapid, but it is worth taking a look at beforehand.

Antietam Creek dumps into the Potomac River about two hundred yards below this road bridge. Take out at the mouth, on the right; your take-out requires you to carry your boats and gear about one hundred yards along the towpath in an upriver direction to your car. This is when you should remember where your keys are!

Directions

From Baltimore or Washington, DC, take I-70 west. Take exit 35, Route 66, south. Go 3.6 miles, then turn right on Mill Point Road. Go

2.2 miles, then turn right on Route 68, Lappans Road. Go 1.8 miles to Devil's Backbone Park.

To get to the take-out from Devil's Backbone Park, take Route 68 in a northeasterly direction, upstream as the creek flows. At Route 65, turn left. In the town of Sharpsburg, turn left on Route 34, Main Street. Go one block and turn left on Harpers Ferry Road. Follow this road to the take-out near where Antietam Creek flows into the Potomac River.

Other Outdoor Recreational Opportunities Nearby

The C&O canal towpath is nearby, with 184.5 miles of excellent cycling, walking, backpacking, birding, and botanizing. Paddling on the Potomac near Antietam Creek is also fun, especially at summer low water. It is described elsewhere in this book as "Dam Number 4 Cave."

DRAGONFLIES

Dragonflies are familiar insects of ponds, rivers, and freshwater marshes, patrolling the airspace above the water on four large, horizontally held transparent wings, with a robust, often brightly colored body and prominent compound eyes. These are fierce predators, taking all sorts of airborne insect prey, including mosquitoes(!), flies, midges, bees, and even butterflies. Being so conspicuous, dragonflies can be quite entertaining to watch. What few people appreciate, however, is that some species of dragonfly, including four commonly found in Maryland, are migratory, traveling hundreds or even thousands of miles.

The champion migrator is the aptly named wandering glider, one population of which migrates between India and East Africa, about 2,000 miles over water, making use of monsoonal winds to aid their journey. Here in North America, at least 9 of our 326 dragonfly species migrate, using the same flyways that birds use, following rivers, coastlines, and mountain ridgelines. Just like birds, dragonflies feed voraciously before departure to build up fat reserves, wait for favorable winds, and migrate in a saltatory fashion with many intermediate stopovers. Unlike many birds, dragonflies migrate during daylight hours, averaging almost forty miles each day. However, this exposes them to predation; kestrels, merlins, kites, and Swainson's hawks all exact a toll during migration.

Green darners are very common dragonflies, found in every county of Maryland. They have two populations. One, like the majority of dragonfly species, spends most of the year as larvae, feeding in the bottoms of streams and ponds, emerging for only a month or two in late spring to breed. The other population has a shortened larval stage—about 2 months—followed by transformation into adults that migrate in August. These dragonflies repeat the life cycle far to our south during the shorter days of the year, thus fitting in two generations annually. That one species preserves both kinds of life cycles implies there is some reproductive advantage to each strategy.

If you have built a backyard pond that is large enough and has native wetland vegetation, you may find it attracts adult dragonflies. They help to control biting insects and they're endlessly fascinating to watch. Dragonflies are not only fast fliers; they can maneuver quickly, stop on a dime, hover, and even fly backwards! While males contest with other males over territory, they also pursue females relentlessly. In response to this constant harassment, female dragonflies have learned to "play dead," falling from the sky and lying inert until the prospective suitor departs. As the overnight temperatures drop in autumn, dragonflies perch immobile for most of the morning, only slowly warming in the sun; this is a prime opportunity for close-up study and macro photography. You'll enjoy the opportunity to learn about such a familiar yet poorly understood insect.

Potomac River: Dam Number 4 Cave

River Section: Dam Number 4 to Snyders Landing
County: Washington
Distance: 3.5 or 8.0 miles, depending on route chosen
Difficulty: Easy, except when windy. Flat flowing water with a few riffles
Hazards: Windy weather possible; best at summer low water
Water Level Information: http://waterdata.usgs.gov/md/nwis
/current?type=flow, scroll down to the Potomac River at
Shepherdstown, WV, gauge (USGS 01618000); see text for details
Highlights: A pleasant summer paddling trip with swimming opportunities
and the chance to explore a walk-in cave
Nearby Canoe/Kayak Rental: None
More Information: C&O Canal National Historical Park www.nps.gov/choh,
(301) 739-4200
Street Address: Near 6504 Dam Number 4 Road, Sharpsburg, Maryland
21782 (put-in); near 17000 Taylors Landing Road, Sharpsburg, Maryland
21782 (alternative take-out); near 17050 Snyders Landing Road, Sharpsburg, Maryland, 21782 (take-out).
GPS Coordinates: 39.495174, 77.824520 (put-in); 39.491796, 77.804178
(approximate location of cave); 39.501135, 77.779051 (Taylors Landing);
39.465992, 77.773043 (Snyders Landing).

The state of Maryland is sometimes referred to as "America in Miniature" because of its wide range of topographic features. Indeed, Maryland has been blessed with a barrier island coastline, an extensive inland bay, rolling countryside, ridges and mountains, swamps and marshes, well-drained uplands, and flowing rivers. However, when it comes to caves, most people think of Kentucky

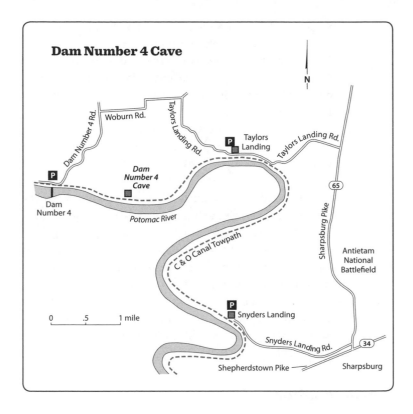

Dam Number 4 Cave

or New Mexico. Surprisingly, Maryland does have a few caves, all tucked away in obscure corners of the state. There are several in far western Garrett County, the biggest of which are preserved by the Nature Conservancy and permit only limited access because of their unique animal life and fragile nature. A few more caves are sprinkled throughout the limestone strata of the Maryland extension of the Shenandoah Valley. Crystal Grottoes, a commercial cave, is the biggest. Less well known but very accessible is Dam Number 4 Cave, located in a rocky bluff overlooking the Potomac River. The entrance to this cave is on public land, part of the C&O Canal National Historical Park.

Dam Number 4 Cave is perfect for first-time visitors to a natural cave, especially children. It is only about 150 feet long, but a dogleg near the far end puts you out of sight of the entrance and any last vestige of sunlight. There are several small rooms to explore, but the layout of them is simple, and you can't get lost. The lowest ceiling is about four feet, so there is no need to crawl on hands and knees through slimy mud and claustrophobic passageways.

Although Dam Number 4 Cave can be reached by walking or cycling the C&O Canal towpath, the adjacent Potomac River is a fine place to paddle, and this trip is therefore described as a canoe or kayak trip. The Potomac in this area inscribes a series of wide bends trending generally southward, flowing evenly between low banks. A few riffles enliven the trip, but it is the serene and unpopulated nature of this central Maryland countryside that lends the area its charm.

As with any nontidal river, water levels must be considered before leaving the house. This segment of the Potomac is never too low, and in fact low water makes the paddling all the more appealing. Low water means clear water, where the considerable beauty of eroded rock strata on the river bottom is visible. Wading and swimming become possible. Getting in and out of your boat becomes easier. So when the summer doldrums get you down, that's the time to head out to the Potomac at Dam Number 4. I recommend a level of below 3.0 feet on the Shepherdstown gauge (https://waterdata.usgs.gov/md /nwis/current?type=flow [USGS 01618000]).

Trip Description

Unload your canoe or kayak along the shoulder of Dam Number 4 Road where it parallels the Potomac within sight of the water. The shoulder here is wide and more than 100 yards long, so there is always enough space. There are no facilities, however. Portable bathrooms, picnic tables, and trash cans may be found by continuing farther north on Dam Number 4 Road to the Big Slackwater boat ramp. (Do not put in here, because this approach would necessitate an awkward portage around Dam Number 4.) Carry your canoe across the dewatered C&O Canal and then down the trail to the river. Make sure you put in at least 100 feet downriver of the dam; at high water, turbulent currents at the dam's base can be dangerous.

Dam Number 4 was built between 1832 and 1835 to supply water to the C&O Canal. Like so much of the construction of the 184-mile canal, it was a difficult task for the laborers. Mostly recent immigrants, these hardy men endured epidemics of cholera and other diseases, floods, and ethnic and racial strife in addition to the usual assortment of feuds, personal vendettas, and exploitation by management that was typical of the times. The present dam was completed in 1861.

The Potomac initially flows quickly for a few hundred yards below the dam and then settles down to its more typical placid pace. Pass under a set of high-tension lines and then look downstream for an island splitting the river. Pull over on the left (Maryland) bank at the exact level of the head of this island, 0.9 miles downriver from your put-in. Tie your boat to a tree, gather what you will need to enter Dam Number 4 Cave, and scramble up the steep bank to the C&O Canal towpath. The cave opening will be obvious in the limestone cliff adjacent to the towpath.

A few preparations are necessary if you're going to enter Dam Number 4 Cave. Bring along one flashlight per person, and make sure that all of the lights have fresh batteries. In all but the driest weather, a small stream flows along the floor of this cave, so suitable footwear is necessary. Most caves, including this one, have a constant temperature in the mid-50s, so bring along a jacket; a raincoat is a good idea also, because you may brush up against the wet walls of the cave.

As you enter, give your eyes time to adjust to the increasingly dimmer light. This area of a cave is known as the "twilight zone" and is favored as a refuge by crepuscular animals. The most common creatures you may encounter are geometrid moths, cloaked in gray and black, estivating on the ceiling. Cave crickets are also fairly common. Long-tailed salamanders are sometimes found in crevices; bring along a small stick to sweep them out so you can examine them. As its name implies, this is the only species of salamander whose tail is longer than its body.

Finally, everyone wants to know about bats. Yes, bats do sleep in Dam Number 4 Cave, hanging upside down from the ceiling in protected places and issuing forth at dusk to catch insects. They also hibernate here in winter. However, as this cave has become better known and more people have begun to visit, sightings of bats have become rarer; there is just too much coming and going for any self-respecting bat to tolerate. If you should see one, pass on quietly and try to disturb it as little as possible.

Within 50 or 60 feet of the entrance, the cave narrows and the ceiling closes in so that adults will have to walk in a crouch. Eventually, the cave doglegs right and opens into a room where several people can stand. On the ceiling, little nubs of stalactites are beginning to form as water percolates downward through the surrounding limestone carrying saturated solutions of calcium carbonate that precipitate out into these icicles of rock. This is a good place for everyone to turn off their flashlights and experience absolute darkness.

From here, you have two choices. To the left, a narrow passageway leads within 30 feet to another small room. Further progress is possible only down a long tube that gets increasingly more compact; exploration of it should not be attempted by casual visitors. To the right, another small room is reached by scrambling over a boulder. Two tight passages leave this room at higher levels, and once again significant progress is best left to experienced cavers with proper gear. Even so, Dam Number 4 Cave is a good introduction to the joys and discomforts of caving, and it offers the only real opportunity in Maryland for visitors to enter a natural cave.

Returning to your canoe, proceed downriver. In another mile, look for a "Tarzan" swing attached to a huge old sycamore limb on the left river bank. Whoever constructed this swing built it to last; it is made of steel cable, not rope, and the tree limb is protected by a rubber sleeve so that the cable does not cut into it. A rider who lets go of the swing at its apogee drops into a deep spot in the river with a resounding splash; only good swimmers should try this swing.

Continuing downstream, the Potomac resumes its slow flow to the sea. Big silver maples and sycamores line the shady banks; hawks and vultures wheel overhead. The ubiquitous great blue heron stalks the shallows and the occasional fish jumps, but nothing else disturbs the quiet. When the current slackens and the river becomes deeper, Taylors Landing is just ahead.

You may elect to pull out at Taylors Landing if you're looking for a short trip. The distance from Dam Number 4 to Taylors Landing is 3.5 miles; that's sufficient if you've spent lots of time in the cave and had several swim stops. If you're interested in doing more paddling, continue for another 4.5 miles to Snyders Landing, the next convenient access.

The rest of the trip is more of the same, very pleasant but uneventful. Below Taylors Landing the current picks up and dances again over a few small riffles. The last of these, visible only at low water, is truly unique; outcrops of rock ledges run parallel to the river's flow, rather than perpendicular to it. This creates several aisles for boats, each separated from the adjacent one by rock fins. Just past here, the current slows, and the last mile of paddling to Snyders Landing is in deep, flat water.

The shuttle between Dam Number 4 and Snyders Landing is a long one, although the pastoral countryside eases the ride. For this reason, consider carrying a bike along with you in the canoe, assuming that you have the space. You can then pedal back to your car on the canal towpath, a very easy and direct route.

Directions

From Baltimore or Washington, DC, take I-70 west. Exit at Route 65, also marked for Antietam National Battlefield, heading south. Turn right on Route 68, Lappans Road. Turn left on Route 632, Downsville Road, which turns into Dam Number 4 Road. Continue on this road until you reach the put-in, within sight of the Potomac. To reach Taylors and Snyders Landings, see the map.

Other Outdoor Recreational Opportunities Nearby

The C&O Canal towpath in this area is well suited for bicycling, with a smooth surface unmarred by roots or rocks. It is also one of the prettier sections of the towpath, especially in autumn, when the dry leaves lend a smoky aroma to the air. Nearby is Antietam National Battlefield, which is a fine venue for cycling or walking.

BATS OF MARYLAND

Among the diverse and wonderful collection of animals that roam Maryland, few are looked upon with as much fear and loathing as bats. These little mammals have long been associated with evil, but in fact a more benign and beneficial animal would be difficult to imagine. All of the ten species of bats found in Maryland eat

(continued)

insects exclusively and provide a natural form of population control of mosquitoes, midges, flies, and moths.

Bats are likely to be seen in Maryland only between mid-spring and mid-fall. In this warm weather, they roost in dark, sheltered areas of caves, barns, houses, and hollow trees during daylight hours. Bats emerge at dusk to feed on night-flying insects, and they may continue to capture and eat their prey until dawn. Indeed, a bat may eat up to half its own weight in insects daily. Most people know that bats find their prey by echolocation, but less well appreciated is how the insect is captured. Bats found in Maryland have an interfemoral membrane enclosing the tail and anchored against the two legs. Insects are captured in this netlike structure and then immediately removed by mouth as the bat curls into a shape resembling the letter C. The bat then resumes its normal flight pattern. The most reliable place to see bats is around the lights illuminating stadiums on hot summer nights. As cold weather arrives with autumn, insect prey begins to get scarce, and bats prepare for hibernation. Some migrate southward, but typically only up to a few hundred miles. Caves, with little variation in temperature and humidity, are favored hibernacula.

The most common bat in Maryland is the little brown bat, found throughout the state. Its head and body are only two inches long; the tail adds another inch and a half. It has a wingspan of about 10 inches, making it look much larger than it really is. Among the other nine species of bats found in Maryland, three only pass through during migration. The state's rarest bat, the Indiana myotis, is known only from two caves in extreme western Maryland and is carried on the federal list of endangered species.

Bat populations in Maryland, and throughout the northeast, have declined dramatically since 2007. By one estimate, more than 80 percent of bats in the northeast were lost in the ensuing decade, and some caves where bats have historically overwintered are now empty, including some in Maryland. The cause of this extreme mortality is white nose syndrome, where a fungus infects the skin of the muzzle, ears, and wings. Irritated by the fungus, bats break their winter torpor and fly at a time when no insect food is available. This uses the fat reserves needed to complete hibernation, and the bat may die before spring arrives. After a decade of this disease decimating bat hibernacula, there is some evidence that the remaining bats are at least partially resistant to the infection. Even so, given the slow rate of reproduction (one pup per year), recovery of bat populations could take a very long time.

In addition to white nose syndrome, loss and disturbance of hibernating sites, inadvertent poisoning by pesticides, general habitat loss, and harassment by humans all contribute to the decrease of populations of most species of bats in Maryland. Although bats can carry and transmit rabies, the disease is probably no more prevalent in bats than in other wild mammals. Conservation measures depend primarily on education and a change in attitudes by citizens. Avoid harassing bats at all times of the year. If one gets into your house, merely darken the room and open a window; by midnight, it will probably be gone. Finally, you can put up a bat roost box, available in many nature-oriented stores, to attract these useful little mammals to your property.

Potomac River: Paw Paw Bends

River Section: Paw Paw access to Little Orleans
County: Allegany
Distance: 21.7 miles
Difficulty: Easy. Flat, flowing water with a few riffles
Hazards: Windy weather possible
Water Level Information: https://waterdata.usgs.gov/md/nwis
/current?type=flow, scroll down to the Potomac River at Paw Paw
gauge (USGS 01610000); see text for details
Highlights: An attractive, free-flowing river passing through a forested,
mountainous valley far from any towns
Nearby Canoe/Kayak Rental: Tom's Run Outfitters, www.tomsrunoutfitters
.net, (301) 733-0058
More Information: C&O Canal National Historical Park, www.nps.gov/choh,
(301) 739-4200
Street Address: None available (Paw Paw campground and launch site);
near 12719 High Germany Road, Little Orleans, Maryland 21766
(Little Orleans take-out)
GPS Coordinates: 39.544156, 78.461541 (Paw Paw campground and
launch site); 39.624413, 78.384920 (Little Orleans take-out)

There are few places in the eastern United States where you
can load up the canoe or kayak with food and camping gear
and paddle downriver for two, three, four, or more days, secure in
the knowledge of finding good campsites and sufficient water in the
river. The Potomac River in western Maryland is just such a place,
and although it is well used by paddlers, it is never too crowded. Wilderness it is not, but a surprising degree of solitude can be found. And

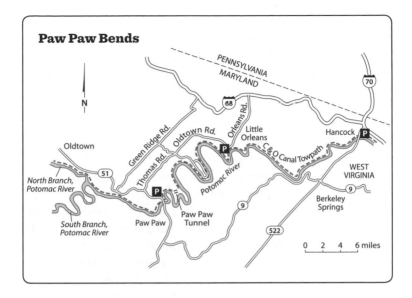

Paw Paw Bends

the scenery is most pleasant; rolling hills, green forests, and little development. Although the upper Potomac is not outstanding in any single way, the sum of its many parts makes it a unique place.

The Potomac in western Maryland owes much of its primitive character to one of conservation's great triumphs. The C&O Canal parallels the river's Maryland shore; it served as a route for hauling freight between Cumberland and Washington until 1924. After that, the canal was abandoned, and large parts of it were destroyed or dewatered by storms and floods. The canal slumbered in a backwater of history and geography for years, until it caught the eye of developers and planners, who envisioned it as a fine site for a highway. Fortunately, preservationists led by Supreme Court Justice William O. Douglas prevailed, and the canal and towpath were made into a national historical park. The towpath was converted into a trail for foot, horse, and bicycle travel, and campsites were established every few miles. Thus a greenbelt of recreational park land protects one side of the Potomac for 184 miles.

This section of the Potomac gets its name from the winding path the river has taken in carving its way through the ridges and valleys near the tiny hamlet of Paw Paw, West Virginia. You will often find the sun in your eyes, then later at your back, and then again on your face in the course of a few short river miles. Progress, measured as the crow flies, is slow, but the idea of paddling is to enjoy not just the final destination, but the getting there as well.

The trip described here is a 21.7-mile, two-day canoe or kayak camper, a typical weekend trip. It begins at Paw Paw and ends at Little Orleans. Since this overnight trip requires camping gear, canoes, with their greater gear hauling capacity, are better suited than recreational kayaks. Sea kayaks and some recreational kayaks have hatches inside of which gear may be stored; just make sure all of what you need to take will fit before you arrive at the put-in.

The Potomac is a big river, so knowing the water levels not just when you set out but predicted for the days that follow is important to ensure an enjoyable trip. Even in drought, there is sufficient water to complete this trip, although you may scrape in a few places at dead low water. The charms of the Paw Paw Bends run are best appreciated at low water levels. Of more concern is high water. Go to the US Geological Survey website, https://waterdata.usgs.gov /md/nwis/current?type=flow, and scroll down to "Potomac River at Paw Paw, WV" (USGS 01610000). If this gauge reads more than 5.0 feet, it would be wise to abandon your trip. Furthermore, although you should heed it, the gauge is only one piece of information you need before embarking on any trip, since it does not predict future changes in water levels. The Potomac has a large watershed, and widespread rainfalls of an inch or more may well bring the river to unsafe levels. Get a good two-day weather report before you leave, and use caution and good judgment during higher water.

At the conclusion of the trip description, sections upstream and downstream of the Paw Paw Bends are described so that shorter, longer, or different trips can be planned.

Trip Description

The put-in is at a National Park Service river access site just downstream of Paw Paw. Picnic tables, chemical toilets, water, and plenty of parking may be found here; overnight camping is permitted. The portage from the parking area to the boat launch is about 200 yards, quite a long distance when you're loading a canoe with camping gear.

As you leave the canoe landing at Paw Paw, civilization drops behind. The steep forested hills of the Green River State Forest reach down to the river on the Maryland side. An impressive outcrop of reddish sandstone protrudes into the river within about a mile of the start. There is good deepwater swimming here, and it is one of the few places where a swimmer cannot touch bottom.

It's easy to see how the sand forming the rock was laid down in successive layers and subsequently folded and twisted. Much of the rock underlying this entire area is sandstone and its derivatives, yielding thin, rocky soils poor in nutrients. Ridgetops and steep slopes have the least-developed soils; look for small, twisted Virginia pines growing here, where little else can. In contrast, the river floodplain and hollows between hills boast a diversity of large, healthy trees because the soils there are richer and retain water better.

The current in the upper Potomac is continuous but not swift. It pushes the boat along at about 2 mph, even in calm portions. A few small riffles, widely spaced, are found on this trip, but none is likely to cause trouble. Merely avoid rocks and keep the canoe or kayak pointed downstream, and you'll have no problems. At high water, the rapids do not get larger but merely wash out.

This section of the Potomac is notable for its many train trestles over the river. It would seem that several railroads are converging on some important center of commerce, judging by the number of trestles spanning the water. But a glance at the map shows that the railroads run straight, cutting directly across the many bends in the river. Trains are frequent, but they don't really detract from the river experience.

Most overnighters stop at the Sorrel Ridge campsite located between the river and the C&O canal towpath about eight miles into the trip. It is on river left about a mile below two consecutive railroad bridges. Although it is not easy to spot, the outhouse and a cleared flat area beneath the trees can usually be seen if you keep a weather eye peeled. The site covers about 200 yards of shoreline, so there is room for several groups.

Camping at Sorrel Ridge allows you to take a day hike westward on the C&O Canal towpath. The trail leaves the river and enters a narrow cut in the living rock blasted out with black gunpowder. Known as Tunnel Hollow, it is the entrance to the 3,118-foot-long Paw Paw Tunnel. This brick-lined tunnel houses the C&O Canal and towpath on its route through the bowels of the mountain. By constructing this tunnel, canal builders avoided the longer route along the sinuous curves of Paw Paw Bends. Less than a half mile beyond the western end of the tunnel lies the put-in parking lot—a handy location in case you left some vital piece of equipment in your car. Bring a flashlight for hiking through the tunnel.

Downstream, the river resumes its meandering, although the curves are now much wider. Bonds Landing on river left is an access point, and a local canoe outfitter sometimes puts day trippers onto the river here. Nevertheless, the river is wide enough to space out the canoes. In the event you missed the Sorrel Ridge campsite, you can stop at the Stickpile Hill campsite, located here. Ospreys and even the occasional bald eagle frequent the wide, shallow places, sweeping over the water in search of fish.

The final bend reveals a beehive of activity around the river access at Little Orleans. Between paddlers, picnickers, fishermen, and campers, there is always noise and commotion—a marked contrast to the peace and quiet of your last two days of paddling. The aqueduct at Little Orleans is well preserved and very beautiful; paddle your boat up into the mouth of Fifteen Mile Creek to see it up close.

A word to the wise: leave any cars parked at Little Orleans on the uphill side of the riverside lot. This lot is covered with water when the river rises to even moderately high levels. Many a paddler has completed a Paw Paw Bends trip only to find his or her shuttle vehicle half submerged in the muddy Potomac.

Finally, no trip here would be complete without a visit to Bill's Place, the country store in Little Orleans, just on the uphill side of the railroad tracks. The original Bill's, a ramshackle place of delightful ambiance, burned a few years ago and has now been replaced with a more generic structure. Even so, it's worth stopping by for a cold beverage or snack. Patrons still continue the curious habit of tacking dollar bills to the ceiling, even if the mangy stuffed moose head no longer graces the wall. Bill's Place is a unique bit of Americana in a remote and woodsy setting and shouldn't be missed.

Alternative Trips

If you have a three-day weekend or longer, consider continuing downriver to Hancock, an additional 16.6 miles. The scenery is similarly fine, and there are even fewer people on the river. Or put in at Spring Gap (17 miles upriver from Paw Paw) or Oldtown (11 miles upriver). However, avoid these upper put-ins at very low summer water, as they are above the point where the considerable flow of the South Branch of the Potomac enters.

Directions

To reach Little Orleans from Washington, DC, or Baltimore, take I-70 west. At Hancock, exit onto I-68 west. Continue west on I-68, through the spectacular Sideling Hill road cut. At the top of the next hill, take the well-marked exit for Orleans Road. Follow this road south (left) to its end. To reach Paw Paw from here, driving will be mostly on dirt or gravel roads, so use care in wet or freezing weather. From the Little Orleans store, turn west on Oldtown Road. Cross Fifteen Mile Creek on the low water bridge, turn right, and stay with Oldtown Road by going right at the fork. Follow this road for a long distance through Green Ridge State Forest. The road ends at Route 51, an asphalt road. Turn left and proceed downhill to the well-marked Paw Paw river access. When you return to do the shuttle to Little Orleans, this road leading up into Green Ridge State Forest is labeled Thomas Road, not Oldtown Road, but it is the same road.

Other Outdoor Recreational Opportunities Nearby

The C&O Canal towpath offers 184.5 miles of easy hiking or cycling. There are also good hiking trails in the adjacent Green Ridge State Forest.

SIDELING HILL ROAD CUT GEOLOGY

Maryland is not a state notable for its geological formations. Compared to the wonders of Yosemite Valley or the wind-sculpted rock of the Colorado Plateau, Maryland is a geological wallflower, where soil and vegetation cover the bones of the earth. Only Calvert Cliffs, with its layers of fossil beds, is well known. But the construction of Interstate 68 west of Hancock exposed a geological site of national significance, where the road cuts through Sideling Hill. Even tourists with no interest in or understanding of geology marvel at the multicolored layers of rock. In response to this newfound fame, the state has constructed a rest stop and pedestrian bridge from which the cliffs can be safely viewed.

The Sideling Hill road cut offers a unique and rare glimpse into the geological past. The first and most obvious feature to note is that the rocks form a number of distinct layers, much like layers of cake and icing in a Smith Island cake. Each layer corresponds to a deposit of mud, sand, silt, gravel, or organic matter that was subsequently compressed into stone. All of the rocks visible at Sideling Hill were laid down between 330 and 345 million years ago. At that time, the ancestral Appalachian Mountains occupied what is now the Blue Ridge near Frederick. The area to the west of the Blue Ridge, including Sideling Hill and extending as far west as a line running between Pittsburgh and Charleston, West Virginia, was an alluvial floodplain receiving material eroded off the mountains. Farther west still was a shallow inland sea. Changes in the level of this sea also resulted in deposition of fine-grained material.

All the rocks at Sideling Hill are therefore sedimentary in nature. The type of sedimentary rock formed depends, in large part, on the size of the particles deposited. Clays or claystones form from the finest particles, shales and siltstones from mud, sandstone from sand. Conglomerate is a mixture of the largest particles: sand, pebbles, and cobbles that occur where rivers deposit these coarse-grained materials. Coal beds form from decaying plant material in swamps. Of course, these distinctions are artificial, and, although useful, obscure the fact that all these types intergrade with one another.

The second obvious feature to note about the cliffs is that the layers of rock, or strata, are folded into a U shape. This formation is called a syncline, and it contrasts with an anticline, in which the strata form a shape similar to the letter A. The forces needed to fold and bend these rocks were immense. About 230 to 240 million years ago, long after the sediments had been laid down and compressed into rock, the folding began. Largely as a result of the stresses created by the collision of the North American and African continents far to the east, the pressure folded what had previously been horizontal layers of rock. Mountains thousands of feet high were formed, occupying what is now the Ridge and Valley Province. In Maryland, this province extends from the western edge of the Blue Ridge near Middletown westward to the Allegheny Front near Cumberland. This same period of orogeny, or mountain-building, lifted the similar rock strata of the Appalachian Plateau west of Cumberland, but the forces were not strong enough to fold them. Thus the rocks in this more westerly region (which also includes the Poconos and Catskills) are still mostly horizontal, although of high elevation.

In the last 200 million years, erosion has greatly reduced the size of the mountains in the Ridge and Valley Province, resulting in a series of north-south–trending ridges. Easily erodable rocks like shales, siltstones, and limestones have been removed, while hard rocks like sandstones, which are less easily eroded, still remain. Thus most of the ridges seen today, like Sideling Hill, are capped by sandstones, whereas the valleys contain softer rocks. This is the explanation for the seemingly contradictory observation that

(continued)

a syncline, the lowest part of the strata, occupies the highest topography.

In summary, three major processes are responsible for the appearance of the rock exposed at the Sideling Hill road cut: deposition (in which the rocks were formed by settling and compression of sediments); orogeny (in which pressures folded the rock strata and uplifted the region into mountains); and erosion (in which water cut away the rock).

Fossils are present but not common in some layers of Sideling Hill. They consist primarily of the shells of marine invertebrates. Climbing on the cliff faces to search for such fossils is prohibited. The rock is very crumbly, and there are frequent minor rockfalls. So confine yourself to viewing the road cut from the pedestrian bridge, which can be accessed from either side of the highway.

Index

This index lists places, organisms, and concepts to which significant coverage is devoted in the text. It is not a listing of every occurrence of a word. Trip names are listed in boldface type. Italic page numbers refer to illustrations in the text. Illustrations in the photo gallery are indicated by "*color plate.*"